Candor, Connection,
and Enterprise
in Adolescent Therapy

Candor, Connection, and Enterprise in Adolescent Therapy

Janet Sasson Edgette

W.W. Norton & Company
New York • London

For information about permission to reproduce
selections from this book, write to
Permissions, W. W. Norton & Company, Inc.,
500 Fifth Avenue, New York, NY 10110

Composition and book design by Ecomlinks, Inc.
Manufacturing by Haddon Craftsman
Production Manager: Leeann Graham

Library of Congress Cataloging-in-Publication Data
Edgette, Janet Sasson.
   Candor, connection, and enterprise in adolescent therapy/Janet Sasson
Edgette.
      p.   cm.
"A Norton professional book."
   Includes bibliographical references and index.
   ISBN 0-393-70356-8
   1. Adolescent psychotherapy.
RC503. H34 2001
616.89'14'0835—dc21   2001044581

W. W. Norton & Company, Inc., 500 Fifth Avenue, New York, NY 10110
www.wwnorton.com
W. W. Norton & Company, Ltd., Castle House, 75/76 Wells Street, London
W1T 3QT
1 2 3 4 5 6 7 8 9 0

✳

This book is dedicated to my precious father, Dr. Leon Sasson—physician, scholar, teacher, wordsmith, and a great man of honor and affection—who taught me wonderful things about being a healer, a parent, and a woman of my word.

✳

Contents

Acknowledgments

The influences in my work are many and varied, and I am thankful for them all. My first formal teachers were all psychoanalysts, and I drew from them a foundation of human understanding that will serve me in my work forever. Dr. Jules Abrams, founding Director of Hahnemann University's Graduate Program in Clinical Psychology, was especially enriching, and the first to model for me a blending of intellectual rigor with warmth and humor. Others along the way— Dr. P. Evans Adams, Harry Aponte, and Dr. Jeffrey K. Zeig, to name a few—taught me different and invaluable dimensions of the counseling arts. The influences of Milton H. Erickson and Carl Whitaker were also prominent, although my exposure was limited to their written works. Thank you to Deborah Malmud and the others at Norton Professional Books, who had confidence in this project from the beginning. And, of course, many, many thanks to my husband, John. He has a profound influence on everything I do in my life, so it is no surprise that, as a person and as a psychologist, he richly and wonderfully influences my clinical work as well. So, too, does George Morris, instructor not of therapists but of world-class equestrians, and an inspiration to me in more than just my equestrian career. Mr. Morris knows all about recognizing what you can control in life and what you cannot, and about eliciting cooperation from a wide assortment of living beings first by respecting their true natures.

Candor, Connection, and Enterprise in Adolescent Therapy

Chapter One

Nothing Matters Until
You Matter

T here have always been a few clinical populations that especially stump the mental health professionals in their service—substance abusers, antisocial personalities, and people experiencing some of the other character disorders. Adolescents could be considered another one, although many clinicians (and parents) would shriek in outrage at these youngsters being included in such a notorious group of individuals. Not all clinicians have difficulties counseling teenagers, but many do, and those that do often struggle mightily. At best, they muddle along through awkward or silent or testy sessions that they later share with colleagues in a spirit of bemused tolerance. At worst, they find themselves saying or doing things they'd never want to be saying or doing, and wind up blaming the adolescent for why the "treatment" hasn't been successful.

It's easy to blame the lack of clinical success with adolescents on the teenagers themselves. After all, they are "teenagers," with all that this concept conveys culturally, historically, and sociologically: irascible, defiant, coy, pseudo-independent, imprudent, puckish, argumentative, and thrilling. They think they're invincible and infallible. What do they want with a therapist? Even the ones in pain can't comfortably accept the benevolent overtures of a kind adult, whose assistance reminds them too much of their own vulnerability and need for grown-up comfort and support.

Or can they?

❋

The Need for a Teen-Sensitive Approach

Sure, these kids can accept adult comfort and support, and they'd probably do it more easily and more frequently if approached by the clinical community in ways different from those commonly practiced. These adolescents—part kid, part young adult—are often approached by their therapists as if they themselves had initiated the therapeutic process and actually wanted to be there working on their problems. They didn't, and they don't. Many adolescents who do want to resolve their problems can't make that known directly and choose instead to absorb the benefits of therapy on the sly; they make the first changes outside of session time, out of the therapist's or parent's eye, without public acknowledgment, without direct comment. It's their way of saving face, and we need to let them do it that way.

Therapists who have trouble working with teenagers don't let them do it that way. They instead demand direct, verbal responses that are already apparent in the teenagers' body language and expression. *I've already told you the answer*, thinks the adolescent boy. *I've already said okay. Don't make me say it out loud.*

Therapists who struggle with adolescents may ask the teenager to review what changes he or she has made toward articulated goals in the past week. *Those were (and still are) your goals, not mine*, thinks the teen. *I never consented, I just stopped fighting. Whatever made you think I was on board?*

Therapists may be tempted to fan adolescents with accolades and congratulatory remarks when they finally do make some kind of change in their landscape of behavior or attitude. Some kids like that, but some don't. The ones who don't may think, *The more you congratulate me the more it makes me feel as if you're thinking that I finally "came over to your way of think-*

Most therapists who have difficulty working successfully with teenaged therapy clients get in trouble by trying too hard.

ing." I can't do this if it means you think I'm saying that you were right and I was wrong. It's important to know which of these two types each kid is.

Competent therapists unfamiliar with adolescent therapy are thrown a curve when their "safe" clinical environments, which invite disclosure and self-observation in their adult clients, are experienced as claustrophobic and unshapen by their younger clients. Adolescents don't want to be shielded from opinion or judgment; instead they seek safety from injunctions to change, from condescension, from adult gratuitousness, and from oversolicitation. Most therapists who have difficulty working successfully with teenaged therapy clients get in trouble by trying too hard.

A Tough(er) Customer

There are good reasons why competent therapists find themselves uncommonly baffled when working with adolescent clients. As winsome as they may be at times, teenagers present clinicians with challenges that adult clients don't.

First, adolescents are largely an involuntary clientele. They are in your office because someone—a parent, teacher, school counselor, or grandparent—has thought it necessary that they be there. They often see their difficulties as not of their making, and would much prefer to assign blame to family members, school personnel, others' misguided thinking, and the wind and tides rather than assume accountability for their problems with friends, parents, grades, alcohol, self-image, mood, and so on. Adult clients don't as often or as stridently begrudge a therapist's speculation that their way of handling the people and events in their lives might have something to do with their discontent. With an adult client, the therapist has more of a partner in the process of therapy.

This is not usually the case for the therapist of angry, depressed, or acting-out adolescents. This therapist has no *apparent* partner, even though a partner is usually or potentially there. The therapist has to find that partner, without giving chase. The funny thing is that adolescent clients can continue to be as "involuntary" as they wish—no problem there—as long as they allow themselves to be "porous" to the therapist's influence, even if that porous nature is camouflaged by recalcitrance and miserly conversation.

Second, the symptoms with which reactive, angry, acting-out adolescents present can be very intimidating. They storm out of rooms, punch holes in walls, cut their arms with blades, drink and drive, refuse to go to class, provoke arguments, and the like. If they're really mad, they show it by locking themselves in their room, threatening suicide, or running away. Sometimes they attempt suicide. Sometimes they don't eat enough for their bodies to function. Sometimes they refuse to say anything at all but instead cry a river of tears. Therapists feel enormous pressures to make the scary symptoms stop. Right away.

Third, teenagers—especially those who do not want to be in a therapist's office—don't necessarily adhere to common social protocols that grease the sticky interactions that occasionally occur in first meetings between people. These clients don't care if you are more uncomfortable than they are in getting a conversation going. Therefore, they don't try to absorb the awkwardness through self-adjustment, as adults (often very conscientious in pleasing professionals) will often try to do. Adolescent clients may not want to make favorable impressions, or care if you like them (some would prefer you didn't), or be interested in what you have to say. This is in marked contrast to the encounters that mental health professionals typically have with their more accommodating adult clients, and it especially blindsides the therapists who historically have banked on influencing clients through the authority bestowed on them by age, status, title, or university degree.

There Is No Influence Without a Relationship

Fifteen-year-old Julie was ushered into my office by her unstrung parents. It was our first meeting.

"We need you to talk to Julie about her smoking. She started smoking cigarettes this summer and she won't listen to us. She also needs to have a better attitude toward school this year," Julie's mother implored.

"Why is she going to listen to me any more than she would you?" I asked.

"Because you're a therapist."

"I'm a therapist who's still a stranger. Besides, she already knows all the facts about smoking and school anyway."

"Well, what'd we come here for then?" Julie's dad asked.

I offered to explain how I thought I *could* help. I told Julie's parents that I wouldn't be effective with their daughter were I to try and muscle a point across. I told them that I saw my job as engendering some measure of curiosity within Julie for what I might say, and that I wasn't even sure what that was yet because I didn't know what things made it easier or harder for her to change her habits and attitudes. Without knowing that, I could only deliver the same old lecture she'd been hearing from everyone else. Julie's parents listened and understood. Julie listened too, although she pretended not to.

"If I can find some way to *matter* to your daughter through understanding her differently, then what I say to her can matter."

The assumption (or hope) that a therapist can influence genuine change within a reluctant teenaged client in the absence of a meaningful relationship is a problem that rests behind many disappointing interactions between therapist and client. The therapist either acts as if the teenager were interested in the encounter, or sustains an unwarranted belief in the power of rationality or common sense to transform the youngster's thoughts and feelings: *This time she'll see how she's messing up her life. I'm making it so obvious.*

> The assumption (or hope) that a therapist can influence genuine change within a reluctant teenaged client in the absence of a meaningful relationship is a problem that rests behind many disappointing interactions between therapist and client.

But is it really that obvious to her? And even if it were, what is there about it to induce the adolescent to change? It's still the same old message in a new presentation—the well-meaning therapist reduced to no more than a hired gun.

This means that as a community of clinicians we can focus on proffering a different and more influential message to our adolescent clients, or that we can focus on building a more compelling relationship between them and us. Or both.

A Different Message

A different message could be something the adolescent hasn't been told about herself before. It could be something she has heard, but never in a way that affected her and made her want to know more. Maybe it's some remark or question or physical expression that invites the adolescent's participation in a way she never experienced before. It won't be an interpretation of her motives or behaviors, which usually interests the therapist but not the teenager, nor will a summation of data or potential consequences have the desired effect. It appears to me that the further the therapist's overture or comment strays from directly relating to the relationship, and the more it approximates an injunction to change, the less it facilitates the teenager's engagement in therapy. The unexpected absence of manipulation, and presence of commitment to the working alliance in formation, both serve to create an atmosphere in which young clients—so sensitive by now to the efforts of adults to get them to change—unwittingly allow themselves to "use" the therapist's comments in a therapeutic way.

"I wish I knew how to convince you to give this another try without sounding like a salesperson," I say to a reluctant new client with a history of negative therapy experiences. That statement is about my experience of the teen in the moment. It does not ask her to do anything different; it speaks to my wish that I could do something different. It is very different from saying to the teenager that I really think she should give the therapy a try. That I do is implicit, but not called for. It's a decision the client must make for herself, and the way I speak lets her know I understand this.

"Eric, you're so bent on being right that I don't think you'd consider a better alternative even if you thought of it yourself!" I remark to a likeable but utterly self-righteous 17-year-old who thinks he has the world all figured out. I'm not asking him to reflect on his self-righteousness nor discern its origins. I'm not even asking him to become less self-righteous. Instead, I'm showing him where it limits him. Whether he does anything about it is up to him, and

the lovely irony of it all is that because my comment respects that the choice of changing is so thoroughly and exclusively his, the boy remains (or becomes) psychologically liberated to do so.

But there's something else happening here as well. When the therapist's remark is stripped of any frank injunction to change, the teenager tolerates—and also becomes interested in—listening to things about his person without defensiveness or protest. He becomes genuinely curious about how a benevolent, nondemanding other sees him. This opens the door for the therapist to accomplish a real clinical feat, that of making the indisputable (about the teenager) acceptable (to the teenager).

The Power of Permission in Psychotherapy©

My first lesson in the paradoxical power of giving permission came to me when I was 10 years old. Invited to sleep over at my best friend's house, but suffering from the malady of childhood homesickness, I wrestled with whether or not to go and risk facing once again the shame of needing my mother to be called at 11:00 at night to retrieve me. But the Shetland pony in Kathy's backyard and the prospect of meeting her adorable older brother won me over, and I marshaled up the courage to try again.

I walked up to Kathy's front door with my mom in tow on that Friday afternoon, and waited for what always happened. I waited for my friend's mom to tell me how much fun I was going to have that evening, and for the pressure of the mom's promise to me that I'd never get homesick at their home. I'd invariably disappoint.

But Kathy's mother did something different. She brought me in through the doorway, turned to my mother, and calmly said "Goodbye for now, Mrs. Sasson, I'll probably be seeing you later on!" And I stared up at this brilliant woman who had become the first person ever to give me permission to be homesick. And because I walked around all afternoon and evening thinking to myself that I could get homesick any old time I felt like it, and that it would be okay and even expected, I never once felt it come on. My mom stayed home for the first time.

Permitting someone ownership of his or her beliefs, impulses, defenses, *and their consequences* in your presence, without applying any pressure on the person to change, is a powerful phenomenon for encouraging the very change never asked for. It's a concept close to Carl Rogers's* unconditional regard, but more active in its appreciation of people's (felt) needs to stay as they are even when negative consequences are apparent or severe. Never manipulative, never designed specifically for change nor offered up in the spirit of paradoxical injunction, the act of respecting individuals' propriety and control over their being and the choices they make serves naturally to liberate them from the need to defend, promulgate, or otherwise impose these choices. In the absence of threat, an individual is freer to evaluate what is working and what isn't, and make changes pleasurably experienced as autonomous.

True Change Agents in Adolescent Therapy

It's typically not the mandate, the insight, nor the therapist's compelling common sense that induces change in most adolescent clients. Often the threat of meaningful consequences imposed by newly empowered parents can do the job, and

---

*Rogers, C. R. (1979). *Client-centered therapy* (Rev. ed.). New York: Houghton Mifflin.

sometimes the parents need to let that be good enough; too many want attitude change when they need to settle for behavioral change, at least in the beginning. But occasionally it's something else that moves teenaged clients enough emotionally so that they genuinely want to do things or become willing to see things differently.

One of the things that can accomplish this is creating a therapeutic relationship and interpersonal atmosphere where the therapist finds that he or she has received "permission" from the teenager to say things to her that others in her life have never been permitted to say. This kind of permission has little to do with whether or not the teenager wants to hear something, only that she *will allow herself to be constructively affected by it*, without refutation, without defensiveness, without bracing. She accepts the therapist's benevolence as well as the therapist's expertise and takes the message home. The client may pretend, for the moment, that the comment was insignificant, but stops short of dismissing it out of hand.

What kinds of things? Things that others, mainly adults, have felt they couldn't say for fear of reprisal, or have not known how to say, or haven't known that they need saying. They are things that concern the adolescent's personality, relations, sensitivities, vulnerabilities, or hidden strengths. They are things that affect profoundly what is or is not happening in the young person's life. They are the things that everyone has been thinking but no one has dared to speak out about.

That's rarely the whole therapy; usually the process is complemented by instilling the necessary behavioral controls, restructuring the family system, authorizing parents to act as parents *or* getting them to be less dogmatic and authoritarian, managing depression or anxiety or impulsivity, supporting school-based interventions, engendering a greater sense of compassion within family members for all of their struggles, illuminating and resolving power struggles, enhancing communication, and similar interventions, depending on what is relevant for each particular family. But creating environments where the teenaged client will listen to what he's never let anyone tell him before is also important, and is a critical aspect of the therapy's having heart. The therapist leads the way in helping the teenager, with or without his family, experience a degree of candor, compassion, and commitment to honorable behavior that encourages a more positive way for that person to present himself and relate to others in his world.

> Creating environments where the teenager will listen to what he's never let anyone tell him before is an important piece of this therapy.

❉

A Different Relationship

Here's how I heard the story that family therapist Carl Whitaker* is said to have told.

A man is found by his townspeople at the top of a bridge. He is threatening to jump off to his death. The police commissioner arrives, takes his bullhorn in hand, and orders the man to come down.

"No!" responds the man.

"C'mon, you're making a mistake. You've got family, friends who love you," tries the commissioner.

The man on the bridge ignores him and takes a step toward the edge of the bridge.

---

*Neill, J. R., & Kniskern, D. P. (Eds.). (1982). *From psyche to system: The evolving therapy of Carl Whitaker.* New York: Guilford.

"Don't do this. Think of your wife!" the commissioner screams out.

"I'm a lousy husband. She'll be better off without me."

"Think of your kids!"

"I'm a lousy father, too."

"Get down you son of a bitch or I'll shoot!" the commissioner, in desperate exasperation, shouts. The man on the bridge looks down at the police commissioner, and comes down.

Being real works. When people disguise their true feelings and reactions of the moment, they lose emotional contact with those around them. And when the contact goes, so does the ability to influence. When people *are* what they feel—which is different from acting on how they feel—they can affect those around them profoundly. That man on the bridge, without having to think about it, knew when the police commissioner's relating to him switched from official to genuine. He only responded in kind.

This is one reason why adolescents frequently get so angry with their therapists and counselors and parents. When these adults are all so busy trying to keep things "calmed down" or under control, or keep the adolescent levelheaded, the kid goes ballistic. The adults find it hard to meld their role of the rational, wise helper with their reactivity to what is going on in the moment. They feel anxious or frightened or angry, but believe they can't show it. They want to shout, "I feel like I'm losing any ability to influence you and it scares the daylights out of me," or, "I'm so angry at you that I can hardly stand to talk, but you're too important to me not to," but they believe that parents and counselors and therapists don't say those kinds of things. These adults try to stay calm themselves, and wind up instead with heartburn or headaches or anxiety attacks. The teenager wants only the authentication and contact; in its illusory absence, she reacts in the only way she feels she can—dramatically.

Years ago, I worked in a residential treatment center for emotionally disturbed adolescents. I walked down the hall one day and knocked on the door of a colleague's office. I had wanted to invite her to lunch. Nell opened the door a crack and whispered to me that she had someone in session with her. I said fine, and that if she were free in the next little while to give me a knock and we could go to lunch. Behind Nell in the background was a young boy of 13 or so, sitting solemnly and stiffly in a chair. Nell looked terribly self-conscious and swiftly closed the door. I realized during my stroll back to my office that I had become, to Nell, the "contaminant" to her "treatment" that she always was on guard against. I thought back to some of our conversations about therapy, in which I would talk about prompting these young clients to reconsider choices made or about laughing with them about a funny story from school, and she would talk about parameters and neutrality. No wonder she felt blindsided by my lunch invitation during her session. Nell apparently considered that her client learning her lunchtime habits and the company she kept had compromised her holding environment. But how easily will that kind of clinical atmosphere facilitate such a boy's comfort with, and utilization of, therapy?

In another instance, my supervisee came to me describing the withholding, sullen silence of a 15-year-old boy brought in for therapy by his parents because of declining grades, depression, and pot smoking. The kid came alive only, and barely, when Rich discussed music, vacations, sports, and the like. But their conversations went nowhere, with Rich trying hard to make something happen, and Billy trying at nothing at all. Rich wanted to know what else he could try to get the kid to talk. I responded, "Tell him you feel like a salesman on commission selling a conversation. Tell him that you don't want to be reduced to talking about cars in order to get a smidgen of interest out of him, but that you're stuck and you don't want to stare at the walls for a half-hour every week. Ask him what he really wants out of this, or if he wants anything at all."

"What if he says he wants nothing at all?" Rich asked.

"Then at least you know where you stand and the two of you don't have to fake it anymore. It's not that asking him is going to cause him to feel that way. It's better that it be out in the open. Then, either your client has to find a way to make your time together useful to him or you bring the parents in. I'm sure they'll have plenty of ideas for what to do with the time. But don't start feeling as though you need to work so hard to get his interest that you start dreading his sessions. It is *his* therapy, after all."

"I feel like I should be giving him advice or something," Rich replied.

"He doesn't want your advice. If you give it, he'll see that you don't understand him or his communication to you. Deal with his communication first—which is *I don't want to be here and have no use for this or you*—and then you have a crack at something real happening. The therapy can only come out of that real contact, even if it's about not wanting therapy. Learning about relating genuinely *is* the therapy here."

That seems to be the difference between psychotherapy and teaching. Therapy changes people through an experience, whereas teaching does so through imparting knowledge or skills. When a therapist offers unsolicited, unwelcome advice to a client, he declares a loss of faith in his ability to influence his client. The setting then changes, and the therapeutic contact is reduced to one between dispenser of information and unwilling learner. The process grinds to an uneasy, paralytic halt.

❀

The Importance of Saving Face

Many of the more challenging adolescents who wind up in our offices would truly like things to be different in their lives, despite reluctant, aloof, or irascible presentations. They want less conflict, less anger, less sadness, less confusion, and less alienation from their brothers and sisters and parents. One common problem is that they haven't yet discovered how to do this on their own; another common problem is that they haven't been provided with ways to do it that respect their dire need to save face while making changes in their lives. It's easy to forget that these kids have probably spent months, maybe a year or more, justifying and defending their way of viewing the world and their own role (or lack thereof) in their life's successes and failures. They need an exit strategy that keeps intact their fragile sense of dignity and autonomy so that they can move away from their defunct ideology and toward something they may only be able to acknowledge privately as being more advantageous.

> Adolescents need help from therapists in finding exit strategies from their problems that keep intact their sense of dignity.

A good therapy helps the adolescent find this. The surprise and relief on the adolescent's face is spectacular when she realizes that the therapist understands this need of hers and can help her both find a way to resolve her problems— be they familial, social, habit-related, school-based, or otherwise—and do it in a way that preserves her self-esteem.

There are few better ways of making oneself matter than to really understand another's unarticulated, largely unrecognized emotional needs, and constructively address them without making the person uncomfortable for having had them in the first place. Accepting and accommodating to this particular need in the teenager works to release the young client from her predicament; somber examination with the intent of dissolution makes it rise up like an angry pimple.

I'd been seeing Maggie for a few months before we bumped up against this issue. She had been brought to me for therapy by her parents, who were rightfully concerned about her moribund manner, darkly sarcastic humor, and social isolation. Maggie disdained anything bright and positive, anyone friendly and fashion conscious. She reserved the greatest disdain for the "in" crowd at school, calling the girls "perky populars" and dismissing them out of hand, by definition, as unintelligent. How would she ever be able to let herself to lighten up if she associated that with looking stupid?

This would be her dilemma, I predicted to Maggie: finding a way, when she did feel better, to comfortably adopt an easier-going state of mind and be more social without feeling as though she had compromised the stump speech she'd delivered to me in earlier sessions. It was only through a respectful acknowledgment of her platform and the obstacle it posed to her that I could ever hope to subsequently influence her rigid tenets about sociability and intelligence, and deal productively with her depression. I was never even convinced that she fully believed them all anyway, but that was for her and not me to say. It didn't really matter anyway; in her sad, morose, and prickly way, Maggie needed some excuse for why she didn't want (have) friends.

Not everyone worries so much about saving face. I would have handled this differently with a client who was more related and livelier and happy to upgrade his points of view. I would have challenged his premise at the outset: "No way!" I'd have said, "You mean the same person can never be happy and smart at the same time? If you had to pick one, which would it be?" And he'd tell me his pick and I'd tell him mine, and I'd have an opportunity to learn about how he came to believe this and where the psychological sites of plasticity were that it could be changed.

Lily was another client of mine, a little older. I never forgot her reticence to change because she was worried about how humiliated she'd feel when everyone realized that she had "finally come around." As depressed as Maggie but far more related and disclosing, Lily struggled against her mother's admonitions to be cheery at all costs lest she lose the affections of those around her. She grew up with nothing but scorn for this piece of Pollyanna advice, and so resented her mother's thinly veiled threat of her own withdrawn affections that she remained wedded to her depressive and solitary demeanor partly out of spite. How could she ever bring herself show a lighter side and *not* feel as if it were the same cheery face her mom had been waiting for all these years?

Poor Lily. She never could figure that out. She understood what held her back and recognized that she could define her own relief from depression without paying homage to her mother's counsel, but she never was able to rise above what she felt would be a self-inflicted assault on her dignity, and chose instead to stay where she was.

These are the stories of therapy I tell from the various clients I've worked with. Another therapist would probably tell a different story, even from the same client. We all see things differently, and choose facets of the interpersonal experience that call most loudly for our attention. In the pages to follow, the reader can hear more about what has called out to me in my work with teenagers like these. I like best the ones who balk at first, because they seem to be the ones who travel the farthest in their recognition of the emotional charge and lift that comes from genuinely knowing oneself, letting oneself be known by another, and enjoying the companionship of that moment.

Chapter Two

Looking at It from the Other Side: How Adolescents Experience Therapy

"You go into a room with this person you don't know and you're supposed to start telling them all about your life. It's so stupid, I mean, like, who *is* this person anyway? And they always act so caring and everything and they don't even know you."

—Michael, age 16

"They're always asking you things like 'Well, how did you feel about that?' And 'What was that like for you?' Dumb stuff like that. I mean, what did they think I felt like after my mom and I spent our whole vacation fighting instead of having fun? Oh, God, it's just so frustrating to be asked these questions instead of having a normal conversation."

—Kim, age 14

"It's like they try not to have any feelings themselves or something. I don't know—it's weird. It's, like, they can't just be normal people. I'll be telling my therapist this funny thing that happened to me and she'll sit there all stonefaced. Once I was crying half the session and all she kept saying was how sad I must have felt. Yeah, like no kidding, lady. Couldn't she have thought of anything better to say?"

—Angela, age 17

F ake. Not normal. Frustrating. Those poor therapists probably thought they were doing a good job of being sympathetic and helpful and available. Their clients did not. Somewhere the connection was being missed.

We need a more suitable matching between what we offer and what the adolescent client needs and wants. Even then, there are many times when what the adolescent needs in order to feel or function better is at odds with what he or she wants. She wants to feel better right now; the process takes longer and involves some anguish. She wants the therapist to tell her parents to lay off; the therapist won't. She wants only to be seen by herself; the therapist needs the parents in session. Most of the time, however, these differences are reconciled and the therapy moves forward. What get reconciled less often are the myriad fractures in rapport between therapist and client that take place suddenly and imperceptibly in the midst of what seemed like a useful conversation.

These fractures are variously the responsibility of either or both parties; maybe the therapist was too stone-faced, but perhaps the teenager overwhelmed her with her hysteria. It would have been nice if the therapist had been able to say, "You're so full of feelings I'm not sure I can fit mine in the room too!" But she didn't. It would have been terrific if the young client had said, "Hey, would you laugh or cry with me or something? I'm all by myself out here," but she didn't—she probably couldn't. Maybe it was a dumb question that the therapist asked his client but maybe the client did throw an unforgiving look of contempt. Too bad the therapist couldn't bring himself to say to his client, "Boy, whatever made me ask something like that? Scratch that one!" and the client follow up her look with, "I guess I make it hard for you to tell me anything when I'm in this kind of mood, don't I?"

Most or all of those things can be said—that's the thrust of this book—but many of the rifts that cause a need for them to be said in the first place can be preempted by the therapist's deepened appreciation of what it feels like to be a teenager in therapy. Sure, any therapist can speak generally about the impending collision course between the therapeutic process and the adolescent's developmental imperatives of autonomy, independence, and self-control, but the specific and microscopic ways in which the collisions manifest in the relationship are usually obscured. Therapists' contributions to these collisions are covered in the next chapter, whereas this chapter goes through the set of fundamental and prejudicial attitudes that adolescent clients often have about themselves or others that profoundly affect their ability to take advantage of what therapy is offering them. Whether or not the attitudes are valid is irrelevant, because the adolescent thinks and feels them to be so; the attitudes, therefore, are already operative. The more facile the therapist is at respectfully teasing the attitudes out from everything the teenager offers and presenting them back to the teenager in a way that engenders curiosity rather than defensiveness, the more likely it is that they will becomes aids to the therapy instead of impediments.

Adolescent Attitudes and Developmental Imperatives That Account for Difficulties in the Therapeutic Encounter

Some Adolescents Need to Change Their Behavior or Presentation Privately, Outside the Focus of a Therapist's (Watchful) Eye

This precept harkens back to the issue of saving face. Change becomes a sensitive subject for a teenager who has been rallying for weeks, even months, to do things his way. It's especially sensitive for the adolescent who's made a big deal about being right, or who has been particularly defiant or oppositional in his presentation. The last thing this kid feels like doing is making obvious efforts to change in front of the therapist (or parent, school official, etc.). From the teenager's point of view, it comes pretty darn close to saying, "Okay, you were right and I was wrong." Teenaged clients may prefer to make changes outside of their therapy session, and outside of their parents' view. That means they might walk their same old walk and talk their same old talk for a couple of weeks in session, giving the impression that they still believe as strongly as ever in their original perspective on things, while trying on for size some new ways of thinking, speaking, and responding in settings where no one is paying enough attention to really notice. We have to look for indications of change elsewhere, in places not so obvious as sessions. If we have a sense that the adolescent has stopped trying to convince us that his way is the right way, it might be a good enough sign that he's reconsidering things. In that case, I might ask the parents if they've noticed any slight changes in their son's behavior or attitude. If they have, I'd advise them not to make a big deal over what they observe and instead just casually say one day, in passing, "Nice job with your schoolwork this week, buddy." If the parents complain that change isn't happening quickly enough, explain that for now the direction of change is more important than its magnitude, and suggest they give their child an opportunity to change in a way that feels self-determined to him or her.

I'm likely to say all this to the parents in front of the teenager. I'd explain—to the parents, while relating warmly but nonverbally to the teen—that their child may be one of those kids who needs to make changes privately, without everyone watching and checking. I'd explain that this is their teenager's way, and as long as he or she is "taking care of what needs taking care of" (I'd choose this phrasing over "doing what he or she is supposed to be doing," which could spark defiance), it should be respected. Furthermore, I'd suggest to the parents that they might begin to see some differences (I'd avoid the word *changes* so soon), but to lay low about it so that their child doesn't get embarrassed; we'd see what happens from that point. Then I'd turn to the teenager and smile, as if to ask "Okay?" but I wouldn't wait for an answer that would force a response from him. At this point I wouldn't yet impose on him in that way.

Other teenagers don't change "in public" simply because they are too private in their personality style. Helen, a dignified and reserved girl of 15 who was caught by her parents with a bag of marijuana, was one of these kids who did all of her therapy "work" outside the therapy office. Besides her dabbling with dope—perhaps because of that—Helen had also become belligerent at home toward her mom, and had let her grades drop. Family sessions uncovered the mom's overbearing nature and the dad's loss of confidence in parenting. The parents and Helen's three loquacious, older sisters did most of the talking in session; Helen would not be persuaded to participate except for when she was moved on her own to say something. Her comments were always insightful, articulate, relevant, and correct, but they never had anything directly to do with her presenting problems.

Helen's grasp of the family's dynamics, her native intelligence, and her strong sense of self and independence made it apparent to me that she knew exactly what changes she needed to make. She had to ditch the pot, hang with a different crowd, knock off the smart-aleck stuff with her mom, and attend to her schoolwork. There was nothing she needed to learn from me or from therapy about *how* to do any of those things. Instead, she required a prompt and now she had two: her mom's better understanding of Helen's need for some more breathing room in which to grow up, and Helen's awareness that if she didn't take care of her problems on her own she would be facing the prospect of more intensive intervention on the part of her parents. The latter being a considerably noxious thought to Helen, she chose to handle matters on her own, and she did it well. She would never have been one to discuss her difficulties or poor choices in a "public" therapy session, and she declined individual sessions. Helen got better on the sly, and that was fine with me. If during sessions I had enforced a standard that she get "better" like other kids, I'd have been replicating mother's insistence that she do things in customary form (i.e., how mom and Helen's sisters did things) and I would have lost the client.

Mindy, in contrast, needed everything in therapy that Helen didn't. She deliberately used the time in session to go through her business in an effort to gain more control over her reactions to daily events and better manage her near-debilitating anxiety. She also was 15, but was less mature and far less secure and independent. She sought out contact with and assistance from adults (albeit conflictually) but was comfortable with and never ashamed by her reliance on me and her parents for feedback in session. Clients tell us what kind of interpersonal setting they need in order to succeed with therapy; we need only listen.

> Clients tell us what kind of interpersonal setting they need in order to succeed with therapy; we need only listen.

Many Teenagers Find It Hard to Comfortably Accept Public Congratulations for the Changes They End Up Making

If the adolescent client himself was on board for the therapy and agreeable about the issues discussed, nothing might please him and consolidate the change more than hearing accolades from the people who were party to the process. However, if you cheer on a youngster who makes modifications begrudgingly you're likely to cause a massive undoing. After all, he's making the changes—he'll have you believe—only because you're making him do so. He doesn't want kudos for something he feels is your deal, not his.

Michael argued for weeks that his curfew was an insult to his advanced age of 17 years, and that he could not possibly be home by the appointed time. His parents did not waver, and began enforcing consequences for his tardy returns. Eventually, having lost his privileges of using the car

and the internet, Michael *managed* to arrive home by curfew. I cautioned Michael's parents not to make a big deal
about their son's returning on time. I suggested that instead
they simply say that they appreciated him coming home on
time, and that he could again use the car and the computer.
Period. End of discussion. To make a bigger deal of it ran the
risk of making him need to "assert" himself and his 17 years
all over again.

In addition, the restraint of congratulatory remarks acts
as a nod to the adolescent's making a change only because of
external constraints. It gives teenagers a face-saving way out
of their dilemma of having to attribute their modified actions
to what others are (unfairly) demanding of them. This can be
good enough. In the training audiotape *It's Her Fault*, noted
solution-focused therapist Insoo Kim Berg* speaks about
how therapists sometimes ask too much of their clients by
demanding that the clients accept responsibility for their
destructive actions. It's good enough for Berg that her client
in this tape, a military man who abuses his wife, is willing to
refrain from hitting the wife only because he didn't want his
commanding officer called in on the situation. Berg takes
great care to protect the dignity of her client who might otherwise bolt at the suggestion that he is a man who needs to
hit his wife in order to feel that he is the head of the house.
Instead, Berg allows the client his allegiances to "self-control"
and "discipline" as the means by which he changes, without
pressing him to alter his belief that his wife was to blame for
his violence.

---

*Berg, I. K. (1994). *It's her fault (Audiotape)*. Milwaukee, Wisconsin:
Brief Family Therapy Center.

Some Teenagers Feel That Any Legitimate Changes They Make of Their Own Accord Must Be Self-Determined

If someone besides the teenager wants the same change (e.g., a return to school, securing a summer job, giving up cigarettes), the idea has then become "contaminated" and runs the risk of getting rejected—even if desperately desired by the teenager herself. This is one reason why it's rarely productive for a therapist, parent, or anyone else to need changes to happen more than the teenager herself. Such persons may want it desperately, but once they try to *get* the teenager to make a different move because of their desperation, they've run the risk of making the prospect of change vastly less appealing to the teenager. Some adults are tempted to simplify this into "oppositionalism," but it's really something different, more connected to issues of autonomy and propriety than to a frank need to play opposites for their own sake.

Is it ever productive to invite young clients like these to examine why they so defensively view their parents' concerns as an offensive commandment to change—e.g., "Why do you think it's so hard for you to do something just because others would like you to do it too?" Probably not in any direct sort of way. That kind of probing question will most likely net an answer along the lines of, "I dunno." It's a boring question, and it makes for boring therapy. I think it's more productive to first get kids interested in their own "change style" ("You know, you don't seem to want anything that anyone else wants for you. It's like you can't stand it, don't you think?") before being asked to do anything with it. This allows them to converse about it without feeling as if they are soon going to be told that they must get rid of it. What would anyone do, believing that talking about a topic meant that they were going to be implored to take action on it? They'd be careful about what they talked about. That's what teenagers in therapy do when they feel that bringing up a subject will mean the therapist will take the opportunity to ask them to change. With pressure-free conversation in the works, however, opportunities appear for the therapist to address the "advantages" and "disadvantages" of the client's style with him without it sounding as if the conversation has turned analytical on him. "Are you sure it works for you this way?" is one such example. This time, when the client looks down and responds softly with "I don't know," he has not closed off the discussion but instead extended a quiet and beautiful invitation for the therapist to help.

All this is in marked contrast to the adolescent who will change *only* when the changes are mandated from without. This type of kid stops smoking marijuana while still telling anyone who will listen that she thinks the stuff's fine, she just doesn't want the "hassle" anymore. So be it. Some kids need just the opposite kind of experience in order to make the switch. They need to be able to tell the world that they did it *only because* they had to.

Adolescents May Make Choices and Decisions Based Upon a Logic That Appears Unsound at First Blush But Is Understandable When Viewed in Light of Their Psychology and Personal Experience

Dismissing this logic out of hand angers the adolescent, and disrespects his thinking style, history, and beliefs about the world that gave birth to the logic in the first place. The logic may begin to appear sound once the adolescent's thoughts are considered in the context of his psychology. Not allowing for that leads to unnecessary conflict between adult or therapist and adolescent.

Frannie was 1 month away from her 17th birthday. She'd had 11 months to get her driver's permit and had yet to open the booklet her parents picked up for her at the Motor Vehicles Bureau. No one could understand why Frannie wasn't driving yet. When they asked her, she said she was too busy to study for the exam, or that the time of year was too snowy or too humid to be taking driving lessons. None of it made any sense.

What no one knew was that Frannie had a certain way of thinking about what it means to grow up. Frannie thought that if you'd grown up in one area of your life you'd grown up in all. Learning to drive and not needing rides anymore from Mom and Dad meant to Frannie that she couldn't need her parents for other things, like advice, consolation, and late-night company. Her thinking wasn't correct but it was opera-tive, and her unconscious fear of being too independent kept her from trying to be even a little independent.

Spotting the reasons behind this seeming illogic can be tricky, and the therapist must be a sleuth. But clues to a client's inner life abound. During a session, Frannie said something in passing about how not driving is the only way in which she was still just a kid. She mentioned something else about how all her school buddies who drove were already starting to look at colleges. During another session she quipped to her dad that once she did start driving he'd have to start looking for another daughter to take care of.

In Frannie's presence, I said to her parents that I thought Frannie believed that once she didn't need her mom and dad to drive her anymore she wouldn't be able to ask them for other things either—like advice, or company, or hugs. I met Frannie's watering eyes as they turned to me in that room, and asked her if that might be true. She looked back at her parents, then at me again, and shrugged; it was a good enough answer, in response to which I smiled and said that I understood how she could feel that way.

When Frannie's parents began to counter her belief with the "reality" that she could, of course, still ask them to do whatever she needed, I interrupted with "Frannie will come to recognize that growing up in one area of her life doesn't mean she has to grow up in all of them. Right now I'd guess she'd only want us to appreciate how for so long she'd thought otherwise. It makes sense, in light of that, that she'd have put off getting that permit. I don't think she'll keep doing that much longer."

In this therapy, the working-through phase—where Frannie would have insightfully reviewed her operative beliefs in a myriad of past, present, and future circumstances—was absent, because it wasn't necessary and, in fact, would have been overkill. Frannie "got it" and, for teenagers, getting it can be enough of a psychological epiphany to move them to do things differently. I'm still surprised at how frequently and easily some young clients will take responsibility for changing things in their lives after such seemingly simple moments in therapy. Less *can* be more. This is how I think of therapy being brief: An interpersonal contact allows for a candor that inspires self-awareness, which allows for a softening of defenses that precipitates change. Most of my adolescent therapies are only a few or several sessions in length; when we arrive at the place where the adolescent or the parent *gets it*, they are usually able to take it the rest of the way themselves, or with intermittent follow-up.

Some Teens Feel So Wedded to Being Right That They Can't Give Up Their Point of View, Even if They Recognize It as Flawed

I don't believe there's a person among us who hasn't clung to a point a little too long, not because they thought they were correct, but because they wanted the other person to think they were.

Shane was that way, but he was that way all the time. He so hated being wrong about something that he would do all kinds of mental gymnastics to make his point of view fit the facts. When the gymnastics ran out of flexibility, he changed the facts. When that didn't work, he argued his point more emphatically. By the time he was convinced of his misreckoning, he had made it impossible for himself to admit it without feeling foolish. For this teenager, to whom everything about himself felt wrong, being right about things meant the world.

The therapist who tries to convince someone like Shane to see the light of day will invariably end up in power struggles. What these teenagers need are a way out of feeling ashamed for having been "wrong" in the first place. Their therapists can help by saying, "It kills me to see you have such a hard time changing your mind about stuff like this. It's kind of like the most important thing for you is to have been right about something, more important even than what was true." And later, at another time and in another session, the therapists could continue by commenting along the lines of "You remind me of kids I know—and adults too—who feel terrible if they think they've been wrong about something and other people know. They get this pit in their stomach, and they just feel all humiliated, like they're 3 feet tall off the ground. Is it ever like that for you?"

Some kids may look down and shrug as their way of saying "Yes." The therapist's sense of timing dictates whether to continue or save it for another time. Other kids simultaneously shrug and shake their head "No" as a way of saying, "Probably, but I can't acknowledge that with you right now." In those cases, you shelve it for a while. Some other clients say "No" with composure and conviction, and you know you've missed. Fair enough. Ask how you misread them so.

Ask what would have been a better question for you to have asked at that moment. Ask them what emotion *does* keep them arguing points long after they've been proved wrong.

Some Teens Believe That Unless They Are Able to Solve Their Problems on Their Own, It Won't Count

Fourteen-year-old Kim sat forlornly in my office. She was as lost a kid as I'd seen in a long time: flunking out of school, dismissive of all her parent's rules, alienated from her three sisters, no real friends, boys taking emotional and sexual advantage of her, smoking, drinking, no desires, no direction. Therapy wasn't helping. She wasn't home regularly enough to stay on a proper medication regimen. Her school guidance counselor had exhausted all possibilities for school-based interventions. Kim's parents, after trying unsuccessfully to manage her at home safely, felt they had no choice but to investigate therapeutic residential placements. Kim and I discussed her withdrawal from family, from friends, and from me. Kim stated, "I have to do that. I have to push everyone away."

"Why now, of all times?" I asked. "You don't want people to try to help?"

"Kinda. But then it wouldn't count. If something gets better because somebody helped me, it doesn't count. I need to do this alone."

"Count as *what*?" I was truly puzzled.

"Count as anything. I wouldn't really be any better, and I'd just end up going back to my old ways. If I fix things myself, it will count."

"What if you can't fix it yourself?"

"I can."

"I don't think you can anymore."

"Well, then, I guess I'll just always be this messed up." Kim sneered at the floor and vibrated her head left and right.

"I don't think you'd have to always be this messed up, but in order to change things around I think you would have to consider that things could count in spite of your having been helped. That some things count more *because of it*."

Kim looked up at me for a moment before raising her left thumbnail to her mouth.

Some Adolescents Are Worried That If They Stop Arguing Everyone Will Think They "Gave In" and So Cling to the Point Long After They've Privately Abandoned It

Angry teenagers are loathe to give up their self-righteousness. They believe that if they consent to "treatment," they give up their right to be angry. Another one of my young clients, Jil, got stuck there with her friends, a bevy of buddies who gently booted her out of their band because her bass playing had gone from bad to, well, worse. Angry but missing them, she wondered what to do. "I can't go back and see them," Jil said to me.

"Why not?" I replied. "They've been your best friends for years."

"If I go back and visit they'll think everything's okay. I want them to know how hurt I am."

Jil didn't trust her ability to use language effectively to communicate how offended she was, or perhaps she didn't trust that her friends would take her spoken feelings seriously unless they were accompanied by some form of drama. So Jil stayed away for as long as she could stand it, and exercised a little drama here and there before finally falling back in with her friends.

Something similar happens in therapy. The teenaged client thinks: *I want them (parents, teachers, therapists,*

*everybody) to know how angry/unhappy/frightened/
confused I am. And if I stop yelling/cutting/running
away/drinking/pouting, they'll think everything's fine
again.* Many kids have lost faith in their ability to talk to get
what they want. So, too, have many adults. *Nobody says
what they really mean anymore, nobody listens, people
do what they want to anyway,* these people figure. Instead,
people *act* to communicate. They've abandoned words. And
once they've done that, they've cast out our best instrument
of human intimacy.

Maybe the most important part of our job as therapists
to unhappy teenagers is to reinstate a measure of faith in
their pleasure at letting a kind adult really get to know them,
and allowing themselves to be told what they need to hear.
This takes place every time a teenager accepts
our help in session without needing to bolt
or become sarcastic, every time the
teen tolerates our concern for him
without reacting with strident independence, every time he allows us
to say things that can affect him,
things like *"I worry that other
people won't hang in there long
enough to discover that you're
not really this nasty,"* or, *"Do you
realize that you are having arguments with everybody in your life—
all by yourself?"* or, to the teenager who
tries to control her family with her moodiness,
*"Be grumpy if you must, but you can't keep expecting
everyone else to let you make it their problem, too."*

Maybe
the most important
part of our job as
therapists to unhappy
teenagers is to reinstate a
measure of faith in their
pleasure at letting a kind adult
really get to know them, and
allowing themselves to be
told what they need
to hear.

This book is about finding ways to say these things so
that teenagers and their parents will listen and be inspired to

handle themselves differently, because they've recognized that the changes save *them* at least as well as the other people in their lives. Psychotherapy is said to be the talking cure, but too many therapists aren't talking to these teenagers; they are "treating" them, or at least trying to. Angry, unhappy, smart-aleck adolescents can make it hard for us to talk to them, but the onus is ours to overcome that. These kids can only help us so much in a process that they didn't request from us in the first place.

Chapter Three

How We Wind Up *Not* Helping

T eenagers aren't the only ones with attitudes or belief systems that get in the way of therapy proceeding smoothly. Therapists have them, too, only ours aren't developmentally driven. Instead, they're more often sparked by the same need that fueled our commitment to the mental health field in the first place: a wish to help.

However, wishes to help can go overboard, compromising both the therapy and the therapist's dignity. We want so much to be useful that sometimes we do things that make us not useful at all. This chapter looks at what we bring to the table of psychotherapy that can backfire ferociously with our adolescent clients.

❀

Therapists Losing Credibility

We know that a therapist who has lost credibility with her client is not going to be able to influence that person. However, what makes a therapist credible in an adolescent's eyes may be different from what a therapist thinks will make her credible. Credibility often gets confused with likeability or trustworthiness, with the therapist concerned more about being liked than respected, or thinking that the former will engender the latter. But nothing is farther from the truth; adolescents are savvy consumers, and they know easily when someone is trying to make a sale. They sit tight and watch the pitch, knowing all the while that they aren't buying.

In this section we look at ways in which therapists frequently lose credibility with their adolescents clients. The intentions are always good, but sometimes the outcomes of therapy are not. Also examined are commonly asked questions and frequent therapeutic tendencies, or styles,

to which adolescents seem to react negatively. Other helping adults in adolescents' lives mean well, but frequently
they also strike a wrong chord in their efforts to guide or
direct. Clinical team members, probation officers, school
guidance counselors, and even parents fall prey too often
to trying too hard, controlling too much, or pretending
that something is working when it's not, because they
don't know what else to do. Seeing kids in distress can
make us all do things that we should know to avoid.

Soliciting the Adolescent's Approval

When reluctant teenaged clients walk into a therapist's office,
there are few cards they feel they hold. After all, they are there
largely because of someone's else's concerns, they are probably feeling sensitive about being seen as having a "problem,"
and they are in a setting that is unfamiliar and peculiar. The
social rules are different but not immediately apparent.

There are, however, two cards that these clients do hold—
talk and approval—but they are empowered *only* by the therapist's complicity. If the therapist allows the client to believe
that either his volubility or his endorsement of the therapy, or
therapist, has a stake in whether or not the therapy moves forward, the client can too easily withhold them in a battle for
control. Because there is little that the average teenager feels
he can control about the therapy, he will try to hang on long
and hard to whatever he can. Teenagers often perceive the
acts of volunteering information about themselves and communicating approval for a therapist as large concessions of
power, and such concessions are dispensed sparingly by
teenagers who feel a need to exert control over the session.
The more that a therapist tries to solicit these things—conversation, affirmation—the more the teenager recognizes the
therapist's belief that they are necessary in order for the ther-

apy to work. So, given that, all that the adolescent has to do to clog up the works is not to oblige to sit. Whenever therapists allow the therapy to be defined as needing client approval of the therapist, they have given away the therapy.

A mental health professional's effort to secure approval from clients usually stems from a desire to gain rapport—a respectable pursuit. But clients' rapport with a therapist is less important than their respect for one; kids can archly dislike a therapist but come away from the contact with something if they respect the therapist enough to consider (even if undisclosed) what the therapist is saying. Kids listen silently to therapists' solicitous efforts to "build rapport" and view those efforts as a sales pitch. And, anyway, it's putting the cart before the horse: Nobody really connects with someone who they don't respect. Many apparently working rapports between therapist and adolescent client are illusory, evaporating at the first sign of trouble. What can happen alternatively is that a curiosity about one another winds up leading to genuine conversation, which gets replaced by a rapport capable of withstanding the necessary rigors of therapy with adolescents—confrontation, emotional liability and frankness, and extraordinary compassion. Conversations about cars, music, and the latest movies do not build rapport; instead, they work against the therapist's gaining the client's respect. However, candid disclosures by a therapist about how difficult it seems for her and the kid to start up any kind of conversation can and do facilitate the kind of connection from which therapy springs.

Having rapport with a therapist can be very different from having respect for one.

Being Too Careful

A violin soloist trying to give a perfect performance invariably makes errors in his bowing. The gymnast trying for a perfect score of 10 on the balance beam falls off during the routine. The boy on his first date with a girl who really matters to him tries hard not to say the wrong thing and ends up putting his foot in his mouth. When we are too careful we lose our natural step and make mistakes. It's no different with therapy. When therapists are too careful, they lose their step and they lose themselves.

Therapists who work with volatile, disruptive adolescents sometimes try too hard not to say the "wrong" thing. Wrong things are anything that will anger or otherwise upset the client, causing him to shut down, storm out, or get in the therapist's face. Thus the therapist becomes "careful" in what he says and how he responds, measuring his words and erring on the side of saying less in an attempt to avoid disturbing the peace, destabilizing a misunderstanding, or highlighting an impasse. The adolescent client recognizes the therapist's circumspection, and either settles in for an easier ride than he will need in order to be inspired to make changes in his life or pushes the envelope of courtesy in session and tests the therapist mercilessly.

Presenting Oneself as Too Helpful

Warm, fuzzy therapy and (most) teenagers do not mix. Another way to lose credibility in the therapeutic encounter is to not hold the adolescent sufficiently accountable for making something useful happen. When not enough is happening in session, the therapist in this situation starts trying harder to figure out how to identify and solve problems. She offers her client all kinds of suggestions and advice. She gives homework. She works hard to feel as if she is doing something useful in a case that has evidenced no apparent progress in

A good therapist may indeed work harder than her client but at her respective job—conducting therapy.

a handful of visits. A good therapist may indeed work harder than her client but at her respective job—conducting the therapy. Once she starts also to work that hard at the client's job—finding a way to use therapy in order to change—therapy stops working.

Robin, a psychologist colleague, asked me for help counseling a 13-year-old boy with whom she found it difficult to work. "He just sits there and plays with my sea shell collection while I do all the talking. His parents want him to have more friends, but he says he doesn't know how to make them. So I've been teaching him about how to make new friends and encouraging his parents to set up playdates."

"What happens?" I asked.

"He largely ignores me. The parents set up the playdates but they're only marginally successful. He still ends up playing by himself a lot of the time."

"Are you convinced he doesn't know how to make friends?"

"Not really. He's actually kind of slick and savvy. I think he doesn't want friends. Or can't keep them once he gets them. He's kind of obnoxious, to tell you the truth."

"Why are you teaching this kid something he already knows how to do?"

"Because I don't know what else to do with him," Robin laughed. "He's bossy and sloppy and a know-it-all. I can't tell him anything, and he doesn't think he's got a problem. So I just keep finding different ways to help him make friends. We role play and act out all sorts of social situations, but I always feel kind of silly about the whole thing."

"No wonder. It's not addressing what you know to be true about this kid, and all your well-meaning help is taking you further and further afield from what he really needs."

"What does he need?"

"He needs to discover you as someone who can cut to the chase with him and tell him things that no one else will but that he's probably dying to understand. Like why he gets so bossy and how it's not fun to play with him when he's that way and the price he pays for it."

"I don't want to hurt his feelings, though."

"You won't, if he sees you as on his side and as being someone brave enough to take that chance of telling him things that are hard to tell somebody. It needs to come up not as something you surmise or heard about from a third party, but instead out of your personal experience with him, like, 'Boy, you're so funny telling me that story about the field trip to the helicopter museum but I don't imagine that you'd ever let me tell you anything about aviation myself!'"

"How do I make that switch in treatment strategy without feeling like I'm telling him I was doing it all wrong?"

"Tell him you were doing it all wrong. Tell his parents, too. Tell them benevolently that this is a savvy kid who let all of you believe he needed only a little lesson on making friends when in fact he needed something else. Help with his need to be bossy. Help with his need to be a know-it-all. Help with his tendency to alienate people. You're working too hard, and they are not working hard enough, the boy included."

Therapists trying to be too helpful in the wrong ways also run the risk of arousing a pronounced counterdependence within adolescents who are made uncomfortable by unreserved overtures of adult help. When the wish to help is too eager and made too apparent, it can become claustrophobic to the young client and actually back him off. I think this could be especially so for adolescent males working with a female therapist. I've never believed that adolescent males should see only male therapists, but I do think that female therapists need to be careful not to exude a warmth that is more maternal than mentorlike. Expressions of helpfulness are best communicated abundantly but indirectly (in attitude, facial expression, willingness to listen, openness to the client's idiosyncracies, making useful points, and delivering good ideas), and concomitant with an anticipation that the adolescent client will be an active partner in the process.

Trying to Mask the Fact that You're Stumped

There is nothing so apparent to teenaged clients than a therapist in trouble in session. They pick it up in the anxious therapist's word choices, body language, and timing: a hesitation that lasts a little too long, a stammer, eye contact that is too fleeting. From these clues they can discern that the therapist hasn't a clue what to do or say next. And therapists' attempts to disguise it only make the situation worse.

Jared comes in for group therapy and regales his peers with tales from his individual therapy session: "She asked me this question and I said, "Why should I tell you? and she got all nervous and started to pull her pen cap on and off the top of the pen. And then I noticed she had started sweating, you know, right there, over her upper lip. She didn't know what to say to me. Man, I just started laughing. . . ."

I stopped him as quickly as I could, but not before all the other teenagers guffawed in unison, participating vicariously in Jared's seeming coup de grâce. They all recognized the game, even if they'd never successfully played it.

My heart went out to Amelia, Jared's individual therapist. I've had it happen to me; it's an awful feeling. What would I have done differently? What could Amelia have done differently?

We could have—should have—let on to our respective insurgents that their provocative questions were leaving us high and dry. Amelia could have said to Jared that she simply didn't know what to say back. She could have looked at him quizzically, and asked softly, maybe humorously but never sarcastically, if he liked seeing her get tongue-tied like that. This would have removed any need to try and "fake it," and the honesty in her response would have highlighted Jared's accountability for the brewing awkwardness. Amelia would have been far better off saying to this boy, "I have no idea how to respond when you challenge me like that." She would not be telling him that he had to change his way with her, or that he was being difficult. Instead, she would have been making a statement about her experience with him. If he was happy with that, then asking him to change it wouldn't have been effective anyway. But in creating a relationship in which the therapist's candor and genuineness intrigued the client and began to draw out the same, the hope would be that Jared would find that he didn't want to be so roguish anymore. He would discover that he could get more out of the real contact than from its evasion.

Trying to Exert Control Over the Therapy

Therapists only have control over the parameters of the therapy, never its process. You can restrain a kid who's out of control and you can refuse to see a kid if she comes to sessions high, but you can't control a client's unwillingness to change, talk, consider a new idea, or tell the truth. Whenever a therapist communicates a belief that those things can be controlled—and this communication is almost always inadvertent—the therapist's credibility to the adolescent, who knows better, dissolves.

Linda and Frank brought their fifteen-year-old daughter, Rachel, to see me. The first thing they told me about Rachel is that she lies. Okay, I said, she lies. They responded to me, "How are you going to know when she's telling you the truth, Janet?"

"I won't."

"What do you mean?"

"Either you'll tell me what's true and not true because you'll be in the room with us, or when I meet with Rachel myself I'll assume that some or much of what she is telling me is false."

You can restrain a kid who's out of control and you can refuse to see a kid if she comes to sessions high, but you can't control a client's unwillingness to change, talk, consider a new idea, or tell the truth.

"How will the therapy work?" the parents wondered. Good question.

"I may not need to know what events actually did or did not happen in order to help Rachel. The only thing I can ever know for sure with my clients is what happens here in the office, with me. I'm hopeful that will be enough to make a difference. Besides, if this becomes important to Rachel, she'll want to talk truthfully with me. If it doesn't, no amount of encouraging her to tell the truth is going to make a difference."

If Rachel were to have decided to rebuff my help and never to be truthful with me, then there really wouldn't have been much I could have done for her. In that situation, the objectives of the therapy would have changed from working with Rachel to only working with the parents. They couldn't control her lying, but they could have enforced consequences for it and therapy could have helped them with that enforcement. They couldn't make Rachel talk about herself, but they could have talked with me and with each other about her and hopefully learned why their daughter chose not to speak truthfully. And, finally, they could have used the opportunity of family or parent sessions to widen the lens on Rachel's symptom and pick out any unsuspected themes of deceit present in their family life that would have helped put her lying in context.

The reason all these approaches listed above so compromise a therapist's credibility is that they position the therapist as trying too hard to make the "correct" thing happen, correct meaning whatever that particular therapist thinks should happen or needs to happen, or wants to have happen. Incorrect is whatever makes that therapist feel uncomfortable, unliked, unhelpful, self-conscious, self-doubtful, or out of control. They are horrible feelings, but when a therapist works to prevent them, he winds up doing what I call "tightrope therapy," a therapy where every step is measured to keep it from failing.

As an adolescent, I had curly, frizzy hair when straight hair was all the rage. I spent absurd amounts of time trying to make mine do what I wanted it to do rather than allow it to be natural. Once, after having spent an hour and a half blow-drying my hair one inch-wide strip at a time, and horrified to find it raining, I trotted out of my house and into my date's car with each hand clutching half a head of hair and pulling down in a vain attempt to keep my hair straight. I must have looked like an idiot, and I never did see that boy again.

I know now that I would have been so much better off letting my hair be its curly, frizzy self and learning to be comfortable with that. But that's a pretty tall order for a self-conscious 16-year-old girl who felt she looked all wrong. Reflecting on it years later, the experience taught me something about doing therapy, however, and about illusions of control over things we can't and shouldn't bother trying to

control. It wasn't important that I had straight hair. It was
important that I knew to get a different haircut.

Three Questions Adolescents Hate

"How Did That Make You Feel?"

This question reflects perfectly the insulting and irrelevant
pursuit of affect that sends many an adolescent's therapy to
its premature demise. It is predictable and stereotypic; to the
teenager, it's just very corny. It begs the obvious: *What do
you mean how did that make me feel? Shitty. That's how
it made me feel.*

The other problem is that the question indulges
teenagers' proclivity to take action impulsively based only on
how they feel. A therapist wants to know what clients feel in
given situations; it both shows respect for the client and
allows for better therapy. But the manner in which this question typically is asked risks putting a therapeutic emphasis on
feeling at the expense of accountability. Feelings are brought
front and center, without context. They are isolated from the
adolescent's thoughts, considerations, reactions, even his or
her own psychology. It is the tail wagging the dog.

There are times when a therapist senses a need to help an
adolescent client isolate a particular feeling from a clot of
emotions. However, that can be addressed in ways that draw
a broader landscape for the teen, perhaps teaching him
something about the multidimensionality of his emotional life
and the connection between what he felt and what he decided
to do: "I know it was becoming a mess of a situation, but what
was the one thing you were feeling that drove you to say
that?"

The question "How did that make you feel?" also earns our profession its fair share of teasing. I can't forget an initial session I was having with a 17-year-old girl I'll call Meredith. Meredith was telling me a few things about her prior therapies when she suddenly started doing a parody of a therapist asking her how she felt. "How did that make you feeeel?" she mimicked. "That's all Dr. Smith used to ask me whenever I told her anything. 'How did that make you feeeel, Meredith?' Ugh, I hated that. . . ."

It can be all right for clients to tease us, but this teenager found her therapist's question annoying and inane. There will always be kids who won't mind an inquiry made this way, and a few who will welcome it, but those who find it off-putting will probably make several negative assumptions about the likelihood of the therapy's appeal to them.

"Do You Think That's Such a Good Idea?"

Therapists ask this question of a client when they are trying to portray neutrality about a client's anticipated action. But such masking of feeling or opinion greatly compromises the therapists' genuineness, and something in the therapist-client relationship is lost. And it's not as if those feelings or opinions aren't apparent in the question.

If kids are about to do something that's dumb, they can appreciate the candor (and frank opinion!) of a therapist saying, "Why do that?" It's what they would pick up anyway in the therapist's question about whether or not they thought it was such a good idea, only now the therapist's opinion is communicated directly and the adolescent can respond to it directly. Most young clients never begrudge us our opinions, just the pretense that we are not communicating those opinions. Therapy can't be separated from values any more than it can be separated from the persons of the therapist and the client. But having values is different than casting judgment or making demands that the other person do anything in accordance with the stated values. The therapist is not admonishing the adolescent, "Don't do that." He is only saying, "I probably wouldn't do that were I in your shoes. But I recognize I'm not. Here's how I look at these things, if it interests you."

A teenager may need space in the session to mull that over, and that mulling probably will come out in silence. Asking the client for a response when it's not being freely offered puts too fine a point on the fact (or possibility) that he is considering another perspective. Let him alone to change his mind. *Change the subject.*

It's different when the adolescent is talking about something really dumb. "I'm gonna ride up to that kid's house and shove my fist into his ear."

"C'mon, Jerry," his therapist needs to say. "You can't do that."

"Yeah, why not?"

"Because his parents are mad enough to press charges against you and you'll be a sorry soul working off those fines and spending your weekends in community service instead of in your new car. The poor-luck guy never meant to bust out your taillight in the first place. He didn't see where he was going. Chill."

"The jerk should have seen."

"So he should have. You talk like you never make mistakes, hot-head, you. Give people a break."

Jerry relaxes and settles back into the chair. Because he knows that the therapist respects him enough to trust him with his genuine response, he can allow the therapist to affect him with his words and demeanor.

"Why Do You Think You Did That?"

What a turn-off question. Teenagers don't know. Most adults don't know. It's a question that makes therapy boring and pedantic, and rarely generates the insight for which the therapist is hoping. Moreover, most adolescents can't use the insight to change how they'd handle a situation the next time; in fact, for the difficult adolescent client, the insight serves only as an excuse to do it the very same problematic way again!

"You get so stuck in those situations," or "I'd love to see you eventually be able to come up with some other way to handle that," or even a candid "What an unfortunate choice," all impact the teenaged client more poignantly than asking an academic-sounding question to which the adolescent can only respond with, "I don't know." Most therapists dread asking this question because they know what the answer is going to be. They ask it anyway, because they think it's an important question. It's not.

❈

Three Therapies That Don't Work

Sham Therapy

Sham therapy happens whenever a therapist sits with a passive, unresponsive client and doubts that anything of value is going on in session but keeps on doing the same thing week after week. The therapist tries harder each session to generate conversation, make meaning out of the contact, and get the client to see her as potentially helpful. Maybe she pulls out a deck of cards, a board game, a puzzle. Both the therapist and teenager know they're only pretending that getting started usually takes this long, but neither is saying so. Why not say so? "I wish I could communicate better to you that this can help, but I don't know how to do that without sounding pushy," I ended up saying to one young girl who wasn't giving me the time of day in her first two sessions. This felt better to me than pretending we were taking time to establish rapport (which clearly was not happening and wasn't going to happen unless I changed something), or asking her blithely about her classes in school.

"I keep hoping that we'll find some way to interest one another in here, but I'm out of ideas. I need your help, unless you just want to tell me that you're not interested," I said to another teenage client who sat glumly and stared at the floor.

"I'm not," Ray mumbled.

"I figured. How would you rather handle the problems at home and school your mom mentioned?" I asked.

"I'd rather ignore them."

I laughed, and told him that he'd tried that but that it hadn't worked.

"Sure it did. It was working fine until my parents had the great idea to take away my weed. Now it's too hard to ignore everybody because they're in my face all the time."

"They were in your face before, darling, only you were too high to notice. That's why you thought it was working."

Now he laughed. We sat silently for the remaining 10 minutes of the session, but I knew then that what we had, albeit meager, was real.

Logical Therapy

Logical therapy takes place every time a therapist tries to talk a client into doing the sensible or reasonable thing. Sensible to a teenager is often different than to an adult. The teenager already thinks he is doing the sensible thing.

Take 17-year-old Hank, for example. Hank was a boy I saw in a residential treatment center who was bright, personable, and ambitious. He was also arrogant, self-righteous, provocative, and volatile. Thinking he was more intelligent than his teachers and had nothing to learn from them, Hank began to skip school. Eventually the boredom and loss of privileges got to him, but 2 weeks of making a stink about the insipidness of his educational programming put him in a bind. How could he casually return to school without feeling as if he were eating crow? So he stayed out. Sensible? To him it was a reasoned response borne of logic that didn't say going to school is what a smart boy like him should be doing, but that *if he went back, they'll know he "gave in."*

I chose to bring up his dilemma—I saw it as the biggest obstacle keeping him from returning to school—rather than discussing how important school would be for him. I said to Hank, "I think you've got yourself stuck in a miserable bind. I actually believe you're bored and ready to go back to school but you believe that everyone will think you are doing it only because they said you should. I think that if you were able to find a face-saving way to get back into the classroom without it being a big deal, you'd go for it."

Off the top of my head I didn't know of such a way, and told him so. I also said that it was important to know when to cut your losses, and that this situation was the kind in which people can lose more by hanging on than by letting go. It would have been unwise for me to get into Hank's need to preserve his sense of (pseudo)autonomy at that time. This would only have provoked a defensiveness that could have washed out any hope of his returning to school at all. But later, after he had settled back into the classroom and the issue wasn't so electric anymore, I was able to productively bring up with Hank the ways in which his ambitions were sometimes jeopardized by his need to always be in charge.

Thief Therapy

Clinicians practice thief therapy every time they are more in a hurry for the client to give up her symptom or problem than is the client. Fearful of being "robbed" of a behavior or attitude to which they have wedded their identity, some adolescent clients will hold ever more tightly onto a way of being that they sense the therapist has marked for removal.

Joan's therapist has made the erroneous assumption that because he and his client had discussed Joan's arm cutting the week before, Joan would have made some efforts at resisting the impulse to self-mutilate.

"How did you do with the cutting this week? Were you able to do some of the things we suggested you do instead when you feel like cutting?"

"Not really," says Joan. She is thinking, though, *Those were all your ideas. I never said I was going to try and stop. You just assumed that I was because we spoke about it and I said it scared me. But just because it scares me doesn't mean I can or want to change it. You never asked me if I was ready to give up cutting. Well, I'm not.*

Joan's therapist will probably be tempted to send his client home with another list of two or three things to do when she feels the urge to cut. But it won't help. This client doesn't want to give up the symptom yet, even thought she may hate it or be terribly frightened by it. It's possible that Joan would want to stop cutting but believes she can't because she would have no other way to let people know how unhappy she is. Any of these could be the operative dynamic in such a clinical presentation, and so that's where the therapy needs to start. If the cutting gets too dangerous, then external measures (increased parent supervision, increased frequency of sessions, coordination of support with school guidance personnel, hospitalization if necessary) are put into place to protect the teenager. But the part of the therapy that's directed to changing how Joan feels inside and what she does with those feelings can only be effective if it speaks first to what the client's experience is and not what others want or need it to be.

A 19-year-old broody, theatrical client of mine, Kenny, with a history of severe, debilitating bouts of depression and withdrawal, once described to me how he indulged the pleasurable/painful labyrinthian travels through his melancholy mind.

"You so love the dark, Kenny," I said to him.

"Yeah, I guess I do," he replied, and mistaking my comment for a suggestion that he refrain from that, Kenny added, "I guess I should stop doing that."

"You can't yet, anymore than I could have stopped myself at 14 from pushing my front teeth back out with my tongue after they spent all night in a brace. It felt bad in a way that felt good. You're very wedded to your pain and I understand that. But I think it will be dangerous for you to romanticize it, which is what you sometimes do. Soon—you'll know when— you'll need to be able to leave it, and find pleasure somewhere else."

Kenny liked his ruminations that served both to stabilize an identity for him and keep fueling his deep sadness. He needed much help before he could even begin to supplant his worldview and self-concept with a more promising vision. So did Angela, an angry, mean girl of 17 who each session tormented a supervisee of mine with her vitriol and spite.

"Maybe we can do some things to help you feel less angry in here," tried the therapist. But Angela *wanted* to be angry, or felt she needed to be angry, and could only scoff at this poor therapist's naiveté and misreading of her wishes. Angela and others of her ilk need to know that we are not a threat to their feelings, opinions, rage, or person before they ever will be able to suspend them long enough in the relationship to let us in.

> Kids need to know that we are not a threat to their feelings, opinions, rage, or person before they ever will be able to suspend them long enough in the relationship to let us in.

Many of the problems of doing therapy with adolescents, especially reluctant or defiant kids, stem from a therapist being charged with getting someone to change who typically isn't interested in changing or who has little faith in the ability of therapy to help. Cases destined for the failure pile are those in which these clients are approached by therapists as if (a) they were willing participants (in the absence of supporting information) or (b) could be turned into such by virtue of the therapist's enthusiasm. Perhaps the most ludicrous display of this Pollyanna penchant is the therapist who confronts her client's refusal to do what he or she never agreed to do in the first place:

"Were you able to avoid fighting with your dad this week?"

"Did you stop yourself from drinking beer at that party?"

"Have you made any progress in managing to get more of your homework and assignments done on time?"

The kid's response? *Weren't you listening?*

How Others May Not Help

These difficulties in working with adolescent clients are com-
pounded when there are related or third parties involved who
have misunderstandings about how adolescents can best be
helped to make changes in their lives. Some parents, teachers, probation officers, and clinical supervisors will forget
how differently from their own perspective an angry or defiant teenager will see a situation, or how immune such kids
can be to "reason." These related or third parties can make
unwarranted requests of the treating therapist, and impose
administrative or clinical demands on the therapy that interfere with the relationship the therapist has with his client, or
with the therapy's progress.

Parents

Shelia and Frank brought their 13-year-old son, Sean, to me
for therapy because of his habit of throwing things at his
mom, most recently a pair of scissors. Sean was a particularly
defiant boy who, in the several sessions that made up the
therapy, never acknowledged that his behavior and his expectations that his mom would be more accommodating to his
(unreasonable) wishes were out of line. Bracing against the
consequences his parents had begun to impose, however,
Sean stopped flinging dangerous objects at his mother.

It was going to be a long time before Sean could examine
his outrageous actions with any measurable degree of insight,
perspective, or remorse. Pressing for that would make it even
longer. He didn't want therapy, but his parents wanted a hap-
pier child. They settled, for the time being, for a son who
would refrain from violence in the home—not a home run,
but a decent base hit. I thought they should quit while ahead,

let Sean again have a taste of life without therapy or his parents' wrath, and give him a chance to show good faith. We could always do more later.

But Sean's mom didn't settle before pushing the envelope during what was to have been a concluding session: "I certainly hope you learned something about respecting your parents, young man. And I also certainly hope you learned something about why you feel it's necessary to act like such a ruffian at home. Hopefully you'll plan to fill us in on that soon."

Before Sean had a chance to answer back, I rejoined his mother's remarks with, "Sheila, it matters less right now that Sean is thinking about things differently than managing them differently." I was looking at Sean the whole time I spoke to underscore that not everyone was expecting him to have had a true change of heart. "He may or may not see things as you and Frank would like him to yet," I continued. "Sean's a willful boy, and pressing for contrition at this point runs the risk of losing the bit you've gained. It's not the greatest outcome, especially for a kid who's only 13, but for right now it's enough. Let's talk in a month and see where things are."

Damage control.

Clinical Supervisors/Team Leaders/Administrators

A workshop attendee asked me how to handle his supervisor, who kept asking him if he and his teenaged client (who barely spoke a word in session) were working on their goals yet. The attendee looked at me and asked, "Goals? His goals are to get rid of me. How can I have goals for this kid who wants nothing to do with what I have to offer?"

I understood, and told this therapist so. I advised him to tell his supervisor that his goals and his client's goals were different for now, and for starters he was working on getting them on the same ball field. Were he to have pretended with his client that things were anything other than what they were, he would have lost credibility and any opportunity to influence. This situation reflects a frequent dilemma in the mental health field between administrative needs for account- ability and clinical sensibilities. It cannot always be solved in the therapist's office, needing instead to be addressed in a larger context of how the industry manages itself and holds itself accountable for the quality of its services. When the dilemma becomes adversarial, and one side feels its needs being subjugated to the other, administrative staffers can feel dismissed, and clinical staffers can feel their professional autonomy curtailed. No one is happy, therapy stops being therapeutic, and the client loses out. The industry needs forums other than clinical team meetings for the resolution of these problems, where the tenor can be more illuminative and educational about respective needs than conflictual.

Juvenile Justice System Officials/Social Service Agencies/Youth Protective Services

"Is she talking about the abuse/her drinking/her inappropri- ate behavior yet?" These may be the things that an officer or counselor from another system or organization, involved in an adolescent client's case, feels it's important to know. If the therapist colludes in their importance and presses the issue with her client before it is timely to do so, she risks alienat- ing the client into silence, or withholding, or opposition. These team members need our edification and easy insis- tence that there are many different ways to accomplish ther- apy besides a head-on approach. If, however, it is contractually required that these things be brought up in the session with the client, there are some ways to accomplish this that will limit how much the therapy is compromised. For example, the therapist could say, "Your case worker believes it's important for us to talk about the abuse you suffered in the past few years, and he's probably right. That may be easier for us to do later on when we've had some time to get to know one another, but we should probably try to talk about it at least a little bit in the beginning. That way I'll be hearing from your own words what has been the most difficult for you in all this."

Acknowledging the clinical dilemma in the organizational context with the adolescent weaves the two differing but related objectives together. A structural conflict is avoided, and the therapy becomes collaborative among all three parties—officer, therapist, and client. However, the therapist must take care in her management of the situation to avoid ever seeming to want to work in collusion with the adolescent against the "other" system.

❁

Excising the Concept of Resistance

Blaming teenagers for the indifferent or negative reactions they have toward therapy is ridiculous and unfair. So many adolescents who do want our help but can't work with the interpersonal format offered are being dismissed out of hand as being too unworkable or resistant. Some of these clients are unworkable, but more are labeled that than need to be. Maybe it's time to recognize adolescent resistance to psychotherapy as a reflection of our inability to provide a service to them that is seen as attractive and useful.

> Therapists who best work with teenagers are those who are comfortable with the blend of their personal and professional selves and who remain undaunted by an adolsecent's inelegant presentaion.

Therapists who best work with teenagers are those who are comfortable with the blend of their personal and professional selves and who remain undaunted by an adolescent's inelegant presentation. Humor, candor, industry, and a sense of genuine curiosity help us to mend these kids' bruised souls better than any expressions of dismay over their lack of appreciation for what we know we are capable of doing.

Chapter Four

Change the Therapy to Change the Results

T o make therapy with reluctant adolescents both robust and time sensitive requires a little creative thinking and management in order to get the most out of what little time you may have. Any session with a client can be the last—this is especially so with adolescent clients, for whom issues are volatile and whose families are struggling to manage what are often extremely disruptive situations. We never really know how much time we have.

Variations in the way the therapy is stewarded, and in how therapists conceptualize their role, make enormous differences in how effective a therapy is going to be with different individuals. Therapies that automatically assume collaboration and a client's willingness to change won't work well with an acting-out, recalcitrant teenaged client who isn't interested in changing. When the therapist asks what he can do to help the adolescent keep from storming out of classrooms at school, he's likely to hear, "Nothing. I like storming out of classrooms."

A therapist who wishes to resuscitate her young client's sense of hope or competence had better check first to make sure that the client is ready to be viewed as wanting to feel hopeful or competent. Maybe hopelessness and incompetence are *exactly* the ideals he wishes to represent. The therapy session is better spent talking about why hopelessness and incompetence have so much appeal to the client than on trying to help him to get over a problem he doesn't want to get over. Prying clients away from where they want to align themselves psychologically is always an uphill battle, and any progress that is made only backslides as soon as the external pressures are removed. And what professional interest is there in a tug of war? A therapist derives more satisfaction *and* influence from being able to engender an adolescent's genuine interest in aligning with a healthier position.

Redirecting the teenager's psychological interest in any enduring way is easier, however, when the therapist understands the interest he is encouraging the client to resign. Without recognizing the teenager's current, operative psychological "position" (i.e., *It's important for me to be seen as helpless so not too much is expected of me; I can't stop acting angry or else everyone will think I've forgotten all that's gone on; I won't do exactly what they're asking because I don't want to look like a pansy; etc.*) and appreciating its appeal to the adolescent, the therapy feels random and aimless, steered primarily—inappropriately—by where the therapist thinks the client needs to be. The therapist resorts to "applying" different techniques designed to get the client to change her mind or see a better way, and the client turns off to the impersonality and ineffectiveness of the process.

However, knowing *what* the operative dynamics are is different—and I believe far more important—than knowing why they came to be. Many therapies get bogged down in a witch hunt for the reason(s) *why* someone feels as he or she does. I find that teenagers get bored by that type of processing, and lose interest in the exploration long before answers are revealed. The payoff is slight anyway; whatever insight is gained doesn't really do much in terms of helping the adolescent handle things differently. Its place in the whole process seems better suited toward the end of therapy, when it crystallizes naturally out of the changes the adolescent has already made in his life: "Gee, now I know why I used to always . . ." It certainly makes more sense to the client that way, and he can feel a genuine sense of propriety over it; I think of insight as more a sealant for the therapy than a catalyst—a way of closing it over and putting the past behind.

Focusing instead on what keeps the adolescent stuck now, without the distraction of how
that came to be, makes the therapy alive and
present. It also allows the therapy to take
only as long as it needs to take in order for
the teenager to get back on track, rather
than as long as it could take. More information and more processing aren't always better. Sometimes we do too much and lose the
momentum. The client's interest fades, and the
therapy becomes plodding. More often than not clients
can keep their issues, inner conflicts, and character flaws and
make everything all work as long as they have perspective
and accountability. A simpler and more practical job for therapists might be to try and dissolve the power of the psychological block to negatively influence the client—not in a
series of adversarial encounters, but in collaboration with
him. In that vein, I liken the process of psychotherapy to the
winter sport of curling, in which one team member on ice
skates glides a curling stone across an icy surface toward the
goal, while another team member on skates sweeps the surface in front of the stone's path in order to modify its veloc-
ity or direction. The therapist is this kind of sweeper, and the
client is that (self-) propelled stone.

> I think of insight as more a sealant for the therapy than a catalyst—a way of closing it over and putting the past behind.

⊛

Changes in the Stewardship of the Therapy

Your Experience of the Adolescent and Her Family Can *Be* the Therapy

The reactions we have to a family when we sit with them and
listen to how they talk to one another and to us are not always
best kept to ourselves. Despite an emphasis in our training

that such reactions are for our private consumption only, there is value in the family's learning about how they come off to others, as long as these reactions are revealed with benevolence, clarity, and sensitivity. For instance:

- Dad really is a tyrant about grades. Shouldn't he know? And even if he can't change, shouldn't his son, a nice enough boy with passing but lackluster grades, realize that the problem of grades in this family doesn't stem entirely from him? Generating tolerance on the parts of both father and son—in the father for his son's lack of academic zeal, and in the son for his father's too-critical nature—becomes the goal of therapy now, having transmuted from the initial presenting problem of a "lazy" son.

- Mom is too judgmental for her own good or for the good of her children. She hasn't a clue. She thinks she's being a conscientious parent, but her righteousness is making her kids chafe at the neck. Is there a way I can disclose my impression without making the mom defensive or having the kids dismiss the legitimacy of her concerns?

- This kid considers herself way too entitled to special dispensations. Even the parents appear seduced into believing her reasons why she shouldn't have to do the things they expect her to do. The parents are idealizing their daughter's social artistries and not seeing her as an out-of-bounds 14-year-old in need of structure and limits.

- This kid is rather handily filling an enormous power vacuum in the family, and the parents seem all too happy to have been relieved of the role. How can I present this observation to them in a way that mobilizes their sense of authority rather than causes them to recede further into passivity and nonaccountability?

We are too careful with our clients, and don't say to them things they could benefit from hearing. Commensurate with skills of observation, however, need to be skills of communication. Anything we do wind up saying to our clients needs to be verbalized in ways that generate interest, not umbrage: We need confidence without arrogance, warmth without claustrophobia, and emphasis without overbearingness. We need to pose questions that make families think about themselves in a different way, as the following examples illustrate:

- Said to the grade tyrant, in front of his son: "Gary, I don't think your son is the slouch you think he is, although I can understand how you want him to be doing better in school. But I think there are worse possibilities for him, one being his getting locked in a power struggle with you and turning off to school altogether. Try, for a little while, to let him be a lesser student than you want him to be. Set a standard for acceptable grades, say some combinations of Bs and Cs, with basic consequences for poor performance. Once Mike knows it can be acceptable, although not preferable, to be an okay and not great student, I'm hoping he'll learn to separate his occasional need to spurn grown-up advice from his personal investment in his education. That's the best way I see for him to do better in school without feeling as though he's acting in subjugation to you."

- Said to the judgmental mom: "Laura, I think even your kids would agree that your messages have merit to them, but I think you lose the kids in your delivery. You make your point so emphatically that I think at times it's hard for the kids to swallow. This might be a situation where less turns out to be more."

- To the girl who feels entitled to it all: "Monica, how did you ever manage to convince your parents that you shouldn't have to do all those things? And, by the way, do you think you could teach *me* how to be so convincing?"

- To the parents who aren't parenting: "Guys, I have no idea who's the one in charge in this family, and if I don't know I imagine that Drew also doesn't know. Can either of you help us out?"

Minimalism in the Therapy

As an industry, the mental health field has too often serviced its customers with more therapy than they needed, as shown in the following examples:

- Says the therapist to the adult client wanting to discontinue her sessions because she's doing better in her relationships and business affairs and is feeling less depressed: "We should probably take some time to examine your reasons more fully before you terminate treatment."

  I want to go, thinks the client to herself. *I'm feeling good, doing well, I want to spend my time and money on other things. You may be interested in examining my reasons, but I'm not.*

- Says the therapist wanting to perform therapy prophylactically, for issues he's worried will revisit his client months or years from now: "I'm concerned that if you don't work through these issues they will haunt you in the future."

Well, jeez, thinks the client, *if you stop trying to get me to stay I might want to come back later when I feel more like dealing with it.*

People in other business industries encourage follow-through, follow-up, or proper endings (I'm thinking of my son's karate instructor, my father's dentist, or my mechanic), but they don't beseech. They more easily say their piece and respect the client's prerogative to decide whether or not to continue services. Our clients' wanting less instead of more in those instances challenges our nature to want to finish the job, but so it must be.

I go back to Helen, the 15-year-old described in Chapter 2, who needed to make all her changes privately, outside the therapy's limelight. That she did. Having said relatively little during the handful of sessions we had, and by simply bearing witness to her parents' concerns and knowing that continuing her ways would bring only more therapy and more intrusion, Helen stopped smoking pot, dropped the fights with her mother, and picked up her grades. All that was good enough for me, but it was not good enough for Helen's mom. She told me, "We're so pleased with how Helen has been doing, Janet. She's really pulled it together beautifully over the past couple of weeks. I don't know how, she doesn't tell us anything, but, I'm just glad she's stopped smoking that marijuana and is doing better in school. But, to be honest, there's one thing I'm still concerned about."

"What, Patricia?"

"Her affect is still a little flat."

Her affect was still a little flat. Chilly clinical terminology aside, my heart sank with the realization of how difficult it was to be a good-enough child in this family. Sure, Helen wasn't Miss Perky, but she didn't have to be; there were her three very, very cheery sisters to do that. Besides, she couldn't have been; it wasn't Helen, and it would have been too much, a family on a sugar high.

"Patricia, I know what you mean about Helen not being so gregarious and sparkly. I worry a little about that too, but not so much for now." I looked over to Helen and nodded. "I think Helen's got a lot on her mind as she is figuring out different things. You guys have three other girls with enough "affect" for the state of Kansas. The challenge for this family is not how to evoke more emotion from Helen but rather how the family can comfortably embrace her as she is."

Therapists often feel compelled to put closure on the issues their clients have successfully mastered, but not all clients want that fine a point put on them. Bringing those issues into such graphic relief can take away more than it leaves, especially for adolescents. The punctuation of closure makes it too obvious what has changed, a public acknowledgment that can be too much for an adolescent to bear without feeling a need to deny the change or attenuate it.

Developmental Sensitivity and Normalization

Some of the facts and figures about adolescence and family life that therapists take for granted are still unknowns to some parents raising teenagers. Who would have thought that Ilene's parents would have been so surprised that she, at 16, wanted now to be with her friends on Friday and Saturday nights instead of playing Scrabble with mom and pop? Or that Adam's parents would be so startled by Adam's bur-geoning sense of independence soon after his 13th birthday? Or that Marie's mom would take so personally Marie's increasing need for privacy as she turned 15 and then 16 and began dating?

And even among those parents who do expect these things, many need a place where they can get help in deter-mining appropriate ranges of withdrawal or independence or argumentativeness or moodiness in their teenaged children:

"At what point should I insist that Ilene spend at least some time with her dad and me on weekends?" Ilene's mom asks.

From Adam's dad: "Do all 13-year-olds suddenly act like they know it all? I can't tell if he's being rude to us or just trying to sound older."

"Is this normal, or is Marie trying to hide something from me about her life?" questions Marie's mom.

In these cases the therapy can consist primarily of education and reassurance. For example, I would respond to Ilene's mom like this: "Leslie, it's not a problem that Ilene *wants* to spend all her time with friends. It would only be a problem if you let her. Discuss with Ilene her changing interests and your awareness of them, and set reasonable limits that respect her growing needs for social contact while helping her to recognize her responsibility to stay connected with her family. Have Ilene invite her friends over to your home more often, compromise a bit on how Friday nights are spent, and figure out new ways for you and Seth and Ilene to enjoy your time together. These can all contribute to a win/win situation where Ilene feels like you are letting her go a bit and you still feel like you have a daughter."

Some adolescent behaviors or reactions aren't understood by parents as developmentally or psychologically expectable. Steve was a 13-year-old boy brought in to see me by his parents, a pleasant and smiley couple in their 30s who liked to put a positive spin on everything. All was fine in their lives, they assured me, except for Steve's growing argumentativeness. Indeed, the boy did seem excessively grumpy. He tended to pick a fight over anything his parents brought up and, before long, with anything I asked in this first session. When it was disclosed that 2 months ago the family had lost their beloved paternal grandfather, I began to wonder if it weren't easier for a kid in this family to be mad than to be sad. After all, I had already had an opportunity to listen to how his parents dealt with the whole subject of loss. They glossed over the pain of losing grandpa and described how they had told Steve all about heaven, and how happy grandpa was there, and how proud they were that Steve had been such a man about the whole thing and didn't even cry at the service!

Oh boy.

"Let me ask you guys something," I said to the parents, and turned to their boy. "Every family has its own unspoken rules that the family members seem to pick up on pretty early in their lives. Some families are okay with chaos but not with conflict. Others are okay with conflict but can't stand disorganization. I'm wondering if your family is one in which Steve finds it easier to be mad than to be sad. Maybe this is a family that's not okay being sad. What do you think?"

Steve turned slowly to me, eyes wide open. I turned up my one hand and shrugged as if to say *What do you think, little man?* and he answered me by nodding and shrugging back, a nonverbal gesture I took to mean, *Yeah, kinda.*

Steve's parents looked at each other. The mother hesitatingly began to speak of her preference to "focus on the positive in life and not on the negative." I told them that if they could help their young son to learn to accept and be comfortable with sadness, loss, and all the other negative feelings that we run into in life, they would be giving him a gift of a lifetime. I went on to tell them that negative wasn't always or only bad, but instead was just one more color in the tapestry of our emotional lives. They were trying to understand this, and began to review how they had handled the death of Steve's dad's father and how they felt they could teach Steve a different kind of lesson by letting him be witness to his own father's grief rather than trying to shield him from it. We needed to meet only one more time after that before Steve's belligerent behavior stopped altogether.

Grace and Richard brought their daughter Ruth in for consultation during the spring semester of her senior year of high school. Four months before she was slated to leave for college, Ruth had become an argumentative, grade-slipping, sarcastic misery of a girl to live with. The parents didn't know what had hit them. They pushed for me to see Ruth alone—after all, they were convinced that "she needed someone to talk her anger out with so she could get a good start to school next fall."

I replied, "My meeting with Ruth alone to start with would be a waste of your time and money. She'll probably tell me that the only thing that's wrong is how her parents are on her case. We'll all meet for at least the first session, and go from there."

What became apparent in that first meeting was how much separation anxiety the whole family was experiencing. Ruth's leaving her family wasn't only *her* problem, it was *everybody's* problem. Once they had an opportunity to understand that people will occasionally make fights happen so that it's easier to say goodbye, the family began to understand their arguing as a reflection of their attachment to one another rather than as a deterioration of their affection. They subsequently settled into their last few months at home with almost as many fights, but also with a perspective that allowed them to take those fights less seriously. This, in turn, kept them from becoming hostile with one another, and allowed them even to begin laughing at their defensiveness over the impending change and loss.

Reconceptualizing Resistance

When I was a little girl growing up in New York, my favorite Saturday morning television show was "Learn to Draw With John Gnagy." Gnagy was a kind television figure, able to make massive trains out of rectangles and parallelograms, and gallant horse's heads out of ovals and triangles and cones. His most magnificent feat, as far as I was ever concerned, was his ability to sketch whatever animal or object the children in his studio audience called out to him to draw, having to begin with three random squiggles and swirls copied off a little piece of paper pulled randomly from a bag. Voila! A giraffe appeared on the page where there had been only a squiggle, a line, and a circle. Next came a carousel made from a trapezoid and two swirls. A clown's face from a circle, a line, and a spiral. Wow. From such seeming chaos came these beautiful, meaningful pictures. Good therapy is like that. Gnagy never complained that a line was too long for a proper giraffe's tail, or that a circle was placed too near the right margin to make a clown. Gnagy always made something interesting and recognizable happen out of what he had in front of him.

Some therapies need to be firm and forthright in order to match the personality style of the client. Some work better through a tone of sympathy and patience. Be too patient and soft with a provocative, gamey kid and you'll never get past a first session. Hard-line it with perceptive, insightful, benevolent soul and you've lost her confidence in you to notice and respect her intelligent side. One of the most creative parts of working as a psychotherapist involves this initial matching between delivery style and client. If it's right, the rest of the therapy is tremendously easier; if it's not, you work uphill the whole way. If a therapist finds that his personality or delivery style is at odds with a client, he's better off addressing it directly than ignoring it and trying to make something happen in spite of it.

> "You know, we haven't quite hit our stride in here yet, Michael. What do we need to do differently?"

> "Lydia, you and I might never guess we'd get along if we met in other circumstances, but I think it could be a great lesson for us both to learn how to work together and make something useful happen in here. Don't you?"

> "You and I can't seem to get going with anything. I say red and you say yellow; I say sun and you say rain. What are we going to do, Todd?"

Adolescent clients who sit in our offices reluctantly and make it harder for us to do our job cause us to become uncomfortable in their presence. It's only to be expected, because it's inherent in the structure of practice: A therapist is asked to give help to someone who doesn't want it, or who thinks he doesn't want it, or who has been led by stories from peers, TV, popular culture, and the like to believe that he wants no part of it. There is no other professional interaction a child or adolescent has with someone whose dynamics replicate the therapist/client relationship. A physician facing a reluctant teen can still administer the necessary physical medicine. A teacher's challenge is similar to the therapist's in some ways, but teachers are not ultimately responsible for a student's emotional welfare. What seems ludicrous to me is that the mental health provider/client relationship has never been singularly distinguished from other relationships in a person's life, and has never been understood as one that asks for interpersonal reactions (e.g., client accepting help and improving) that are not necessarily natural to the setup (e.g., "You've been hired to help me but I don't want your help," or, "I might want your help but I can't let you know that yet"). Labeling these phenomena as "resistance" ignores the context in which they appear. No wonder so many kids enter the room scowling.

Few terms are more lacking in clinical accountability than *resistant client*. If a client is "resisting" therapy, then either the therapist isn't making it inviting enough for the client, or the client doesn't want it.

If the client doesn't want it and someone else wants it for the client, then the therapist needs to get that someone else in the room because that's the person who needs to do something different. If no one wants it but the therapist, then he or she doesn't have a client. If the therapist has no client, he or she should forget the therapy for the time being and ask if the client wants to try again later; selling therapy to someone who doesn't want it is a useless and undignified proposition. That's one way in which this profession demeans itself—by its practitioners believing that it is part of their duty to convince people that they are well-meaning souls who want only to help. Other professional don't do this, and it's neither conducive to good practice nor good public relations for the mental health industry. People don't take seriously services from practitioners who are grateful for a client's regard.

Changes in the Therapist

More Aggressive Joining and Rapport Building (While at the Same Time Not Trying Too Hard)

Many teenaged clients appreciate a beginning that doesn't seem like a beginning. Handling the introduction and orientation casually alleviates some of their anxiety about meeting the therapist. The informality is also easier on the less experienced therapist, who often shows signs of anxiety in those first few moments as well.

I don't ask questions that sound like First Questions when starting out, especially if I'm seeing the teenager alone. Opening remarks like "Tell me about your problem," "How can I help you?" and "Well, how should we begin today's session?" make kids nervous. They shuffle their feet, shrug, and stammer. They're not sure what their problem is. They don't know how you can help. They haven't a clue how to begin. Start anywhere but in the beginning with these kids. Ask the fourth or seventh question you'd normally ask, like "Do you think your dad is too worried or not worried enough about you?" Diving right in helps clients have something to talk about besides an admission that they have a problem for which they need help. Another good question is "What was your reaction when your mom set this appointment up for you?" After questions like these you can gradually work your way back to the presenting problems; by then there is usually at least a little rapport between therapist and client, so that approaching the issues seems more collaborative than it would have right at the start. Being comfortable and patient with the young client's silence and digressions also sets an accepting tone in the session. Being comfortable with your own does that even more.

Depersonalize Rejection

Don't take it personally if your client doesn't want to get better—as long as her not wanting to get better has nothing to do with you. If it does, figure out what you need to be doing or saying differently. If it doesn't have anything to do with you, let her make her own decisions. In the case of an adolescent, you only need to make sure that she is safe from harm, but you cannot force her to get well. If you take on the challenge of engendering the reluctant client's interest, then at least be on the alert not to take offense if her attitude doesn't change. Clients owe us nothing but courtesy, and in return we owe them the courtesy of not proselytizing. The symptom is not your personal enemy; it only becomes your challenge when you are working to resolve it in concert with your client.

Clients owe us nothing but courtesy, and in return we owe them the courtesy of not proselytizing.

Assume Less Responsibility for Change and More for Creating the Conditions That Invite It

It's not your job to get the adolescent in front of you to stop cutting herself, running away, or drinking. If you think it is, you'll spend each session looking at your watch to see if the remaining 12 minutes are going to be enough to convince the teen that cutting is not a proper response to feeling angry. They will never be, because you can never control that part of the process of therapy. Family therapist Carl Whitaker warned that worrying so much about whether or not your clients get better robs them of the responsibility of doing just that. Instead, think about how you can make a better match between the therapy and your client's personality while still holding the client accountable for accepting responsibility for his share in his dilemma, and for doing something about it.

If, however, an underage client is dabbling with something dangerous, the therapist needs to take steps to protect him. He is not free to just let the minor decide that he doesn't want help at this time. But it's useless to pretend that this is therapy, unless something therapeutic happens serendipitously, which happens often. If the teenager gets mad at the therapist because he informed on him, then he gets mad. It's a lesson about the natural consequences of acting in ways (e.g., dangerous) that require adults to intervene.

Belief in One's Self to Inspire Change

Sometimes therapists worry so much about what to say and do that they forget how important an influence their own existence can be. It's illuminating for many disordered teens to witness a therapist handily negotiate situations that give rise to conflict, embarrassment, self-consciousness, tension, or the need to deal with bad news. Rather than shielding clients from our interactions with others in an atmosphere of strict neutrality, consider modeling certain adaptive behaviors for them when doing so is timely and appropriate, demonstrating the employment of humor, perspective taking, patience, tolerance, forthrightness, humility, and other useful approaches to resolving conflict. With such an emotionally intimate and personal endeavor as psychotherapy is, wouldn't it make sense that we therapists present with more of our own person?

Chapter Five

Candor and Connection

After years of fascination with technique-based therapies, the psychotherapy community seems to be moving toward more relationship-based ones. It's a good thing, I think; teenagers in this country are in desperate need of more connectedness—with parents, siblings, aunts and uncles, friends, grandparents, and their community. There's enough gadgetry in their lives, and they don't need more of it in their therapy sessions.

However, relationship-based therapies can be perplexing for therapists who have been taught to always retain a measure of personal reserve in sessions with their clients, to limit self-disclosure, never to make moral statements, and to let the ambiguity of the setting become a foil for the client's conflicts and defensive maneuvers. Certain questions arise: What of one's personal experience of a client should be revealed, and what shouldn't? How should these personal experiences be couched? When has a therapist's involvement begun to interfere rather than aid?

We have become too opaque to our clients, and, in our wish not to harm or influence more than would be "appropriate," we have become too careful. It's an unappealing presentation, especially to young people, and it's unhelpful. We need to learn how to skillfully and accurately tell our clients more of what we see about them and more of what we think about their moral, interpersonal, intrapsychic dilemmas without suggesting that our way is the only, correct, or approved way. Maybe it is learning through the polemic, or maybe it is the way that people are drawn toward those who offer themselves without imposing, that engages the attention and interest of adolescents who experience this kind of therapy interaction. Whatever the reason, it seems worth

> We
> have become
> too opaque to our
> clients, and, in our wish
> not to harm or influence
> more than would be
> "appropriate," we have
> become too careful. It's
> an unappealing
> presentation.

relaxing adherences to neutrality and circumspection in order to explore a more active and personal way of helping adolescents in need.

Relating genuinely and without undue clinical formality with adolescents isn't a new concept, but it is one for which there are few operational definitions. It's also easily misconstrued.

"Hey, I do that kind of therapy all the time," a therapist will say. "Informal, tell it like it is. I'm just me, kids love it."

I'm not sure. Kids know the difference between a clinically informed and disciplined straightshooter, and a pal. They may like the latter because the therapy is easy, but they respect the former because they know it can help.

Genuineness in a therapist wanting to make a difference with adolescent clients presenting reluctantly for therapy requires balancing discretion with candor, respect for the person's social space with a forwardness, and timing with deliberately addressing the issue at hand. It is never about making casual remarks that the therapist thinks will provoke the adolescent, nor is it an excuse to speak unkindly. It's not about "letting fly" with whatever is going on in one's mind, nor an excuse for power plays. It's also not an opportunity for a therapist to disclose intimate information about him- or herself, or discharge frustration in the spirit of being honest. The kind of genuineness and candor that prompts change in a client is a thoughtful frankness that sits squarely in the client's service and invites that client to look at herself differently. It is critical that the comments not contain any injunction for the client to change. Examples include:

"You talk about being lazy as if you're telling me you have
a size-10 foot. Born that way, gonna stay that way."

Or, to the teenager who once again rebuffs his desperate
parents' overtures, "You're losing them, guy. . . ."

This kind of relating and talking is really less a technique of
therapy than an attitude about it. It's personal and honest,
and it's fresh. Clients don't expect therapists to say what they
really think. Maybe we should.

Why Don't We Use Candor More Often?

Well, for one thing, we were taught not to. Apart from that
prohibition, there are inhibitions:

- Concerns about saying something that would precip-
  itate a "problem" in session or in the therapeutic relationship (e.g., conflict, emotional upset, withdrawal,
  or silence).

- Concerns about losing control over the session or the
  therapy, or of looking like a fool.

- Uncertainty about what to say, after years of training
  and practice that discouraged candor in favor of
  more neutral kinds of comments and manners of
  relating.

However, when expressed appropriately, candor defuses
more than it agitates or alienates. I find its most valuable
property is that it suspends defensiveness and captures
attention. Many adolescents will let you tell them things
about themselves in this way that they would never tolerate

hearing in the form of interpretations, confrontation, or educational enlightenment.

A casual observer of such an intervention might protest: "Where's the therapy here? How is candor going to help a young client learn about managing anger or staying away from marijuana, or resolving conflict with words rather than with fists and curses? What is a kid going to learn?"

A kid is going to learn lots. Candor and genuineness allow the adolescent to learn in the only way that a young person who never asked for help is able to learn. We sometimes forget that these teenagers didn't come to us themselves. Impatiently confronting them with the illogic of their ways cultivates an adversarial environment. I've found candor to do a better job of pressing—same message, but you don't lose the kid. As a matter of fact, being spoken to candidly is so astonishing to some that they forget they were just "confronted."

Take, for example, 15-year-old Jenna. Jenna was angry because her parents moved to a new neighborhood. Nobody minded her being angry about that. What her parents did mind was her indignant attitude and her demand that her parents move back. Worried that they would be seen by their daughter as unsympathetic to her loss of community, and incur further adolescent wrath and withdrawal, Jenna's parents said very little about her attitude. They tried to appease and accommodate. Jenna became ruder and more defiant, returning repeatedly to the old neighborhood at night, and without her parents' permission. I was so taken aback by Jenna's sense of entitlement, which she saw as righteous indignation, and her parent's tolerance of it, that I told them exactly that.

I turned to Jenna's parents and said that I didn't think anyone had a problem with Jenna being unhappy about the move, but what really stuck out was Jenna's belief that her parents would take her demand to move back so seriously.

Jenna looked at me sharply. Her parents, surprised and relieved, looked first at Jenna, then at me. It seems that no one had ever told Jenna that she can sometimes push the envelope too far and actually lose ground. I smiled at the girl and shrugged my shoulders, as if to say: *Come on, what did you expect me to say?* Angrily, she crossed her arms over her chest and stared out the window.

Jenna's parents, however, came alive with the bracing impact of my statement. Apparently I had said what they had been feeling for a long time but thought they shouldn't say for fear of making the problem with their daughter worse. What I told them was neither brilliant nor outrageous, but it did bring out what needed changing. Their judgment supported, Jenna's parents quickly dropped their solicitous, apologetic demeanor and began coming up with appropriate plans to help Jenna stay in contact with her friends. Jenna demurred at first, then joined in.

The sad irony is that Jenna could have had that all along—her parents truly wanted to help bridge the old and new—but she settled instead for Making A Point. Interestingly, and perhaps as a nod to candor's ability to facilitate and not fracture relationships, Jenna ended the session by asking if I'd meet with her individually for a couple of sessions to discuss 'stuff,' to which I gladly agreed. There were no revelations that came about as a result, just the spoken concerns of a girl who missed her neighborhood and her friends, and felt a profound loss of control over her life.

Authenticity with young clients in the therapy room requires more than discretion, spontaneity, and judicious timing. For it to be therapeutic and not sloppy, it needs an acute awareness of the developmental needs of that client. I once supervised a therapist, Renee, who was working with a 16-year-old client with a bad habit of skipping school. Renee was pretty sure that Kristen actually wanted to return to her regular class schedule—she was a smart kid who enjoyed her native wit and intelligence, and who seemed restless to get on with her academics. Nonetheless, Renee's attempts to "be real" with her young client—for instance, by telling Kristen that she was concerned Kristen was setting herself up for a dead-end future—seemed only to irritate the girl.

No wonder. Renee's candor issued from a purely adult logic that says, *If you want something, you have to work for it*. I told Renee she was losing Kristen because Kristen was operating out of an entirely different logic, one imbued with an expected adolescence drive for autonomy. This drive spoke differently to Kristen: *If you go back to school, they'll think you did it only because they told you to*. Contaminated by adult imperatives, the return to school would feel like a humiliating defeat.

I shared my hypothesis with Renee and proposed that she simply articulate this probable dilemma to Kristen. "Tell her you think she's painted herself deep in a corner—that perhaps she actually wouldn't mind going back to school if she could find a way to make it feel like her choice." At this delicate moment, I advised Renee to offer her client no further advice and instead simply be present for Kristen and what was decidedly her dilemma—and what needed to be Kristen's resolution.

When Renee next spoke with Kristen and brought up the idea we'd discussed, she saw a shadow of relief cross her young client's face. Kristen then looked away, shrugging dismissively. "Maybe," she muttered in response. Wisely, Renee didn't press the point, but over the next few sessions, she noticed that Kristen began mentioning various things taking place at school. Three sessions later Kristen walked in lugging her school backpack, feigning nonchalance. Had Renee chosen to be spontaneous and candid at that moment, she might have expressed her pleasure at Kristen's seeming return to school: "Wow, you're back. That's terrific." Instead, she recognized her client's need to call the shots in her own life, and deliberately muted her response. "Hi, Kristen," she welcomed the teen. "What's up?"

Some therapists would want to know how Kristen got herself back to school. That was never the hard part—she could do that without our help, once the psychological pathway was cleared. Back to curling again: The curling stone carries its own momentum once sent onto the ice, and the sweepers clear the way ahead to modify direction and speed. Nobody has to tell the stone how to glide. A teenager with no real motivation for school presents differently altogether. Kristen's problem was never one of motivation—it was one of (misguided) autonomy.

⊛

The Risks of Being More Forthcoming

When you put more of yourself in a situation, more of yourself will stand out. Therapists who are less neutral in their therapeutic approach with clients have an enormous responsibility to make sure that what they say and do is in their clients' best interests. The need for introspection, self-awareness, and benevolent intent is constant and rigorous.

- Therapists who do not like a family or client may be tempted to justify offending or condescending remarks by thinking that they're just being "honest" and that the clients need to know that bit of information about themselves. Therapists frustrated with the lack or slow pace of progress in the therapy might try and justify a provocative or aggressive comment by a need to get the client "moving."

- Teenagers who act out in session or relate aggressively can bring out strong negative feelings in even the most patient of therapists. At such times, a therapist, feeling vengeful, might let slip a comment that stings. That's mean. Candor must never be used casually or flippantly; it must especially never be used sarcastically.

- Kids doing something that is morally offensive to a therapist may prompt the therapist to use the excuse of candor and genuineness to introduce a discussion of values that is not appropriate, as in lecturing or preaching to the client. Therapists also have to be careful about using such situations as springboards to discuss religious or political preferences and the like. Demonstrating genuine shock or dismay at a client's frank cruelty to an animal or classmate is different from discussing that client's behavior in the context of his moral upbringing, or lack thereof.

- Therapists who get stuck in a session and are unsure what to say or do next might be tempted to say whatever is on their mind in the hope of striking on something therapeutic. This is an act of desperation; it is not good therapy and is never an example of authenticity in the consulting room.

Not every therapist will want to bother with the responsibility of balancing their candor with self-awareness, and some won't be capable. For many, that will be reason enough to justify a more cautious stance with their clients. But it's ridiculous to think that our adolescent clients don't know how we feel about them no matter how neutral we stay. Certain things, like whether or not we enjoy the company of the person in a room with us, manage to come through no matter what.

Here's the funny thing, however. One saving paradox of authenticity and candor in psychotherapy is that they actually help clear space for genuine affection and caring to grow when it's not there to start. Whenever there are opportunities to address the quality of the real relationship between oneself and another person, there are opportunities to speak to what isn't working.

> One saving paradox of authenticity and candor in psychotherapy is that they actually help clear space for genuine affection and caring to grow when it's not there to start.

Take, for instance, the boy who dismisses out of hand everything you've said over the past couple of weeks. You are feeling irrelevant. Some therapists might sit on their frustration, concerned that if they addressed their anger it would come out inappropriately. Others might interpret the boy's rebuttals as his way of staying in charge, letting you know you're not needed, or getting back at adults. Another option, however, is to say something along the lines of "I feel like a nobody in here when we talk, Jeff. If I say 'red' you say 'blue.' I say 'rain' you say 'sun.' I know this was never your idea of a good time, but I can barely say a sentence before you toss it out the window. Does this happen with other people, or just me? Has anyone ever said anything like this to you before?"

This is candor that connects. It's personal, inquisitive, and part of the therapist's experience of the client. There's also no demand for the client to change. He can consider the point or not; he can answer the question or not; he can continue to dismiss what's being said to him as he's always done, or start to engage. Ironically, and without design, the candid comment will likely result in the boy's acknowledgment of the therapist's dilemma, and a diminished rebuffing of the therapist's thoughts. This is quite a different thing from the therapist who stuffs his growing irritation with a contentious kid only to get candid by bursting out: "Just listen to me for a change!"

And if a therapist really doesn't like his client? It's incumbent on the therapist to *find* a way to like her, if at all possible. The therapist needs either to work to discover something likeable about the client, or draw up enough compassion for her unlikeability that they come into the affection backwards, so to speak.

Lisa was a 13-year-old girl whom, in the beginning of our work together, I had trouble finding any way to like. She was miserable, depressive, exceedingly passive, and sarcastic. The little humor she had was dark and cruel, and she related impersonally, using the person in front of her as a captive audience for her callow soapboxing about teenage rights and liberties. She was committed to a Gothic lifestyle and sneered continuously whenever spoken to.

Oh, how I tried to find something to like about Lisa. I thought about how miserable she must be, how depressed, how lonely—but all I could think of in response was, *Of course she's lonely, who'd want to be around her?* I thought about how her dad said things that belittled her under the guise of trying to get her to lighten up. I thought about what it must be like to wake up each day wedded to all things black and morbid, and what it must be like to have opinions about things no one else wanted to discuss. I felt sorry for her, and wanted to help her, but I still didn't like her.

But something changed on the day Lisa told me her birthday was coming up and that she didn't want anything done for her. I challenged her. Lisa sneered at me and replied, "Oh,

I'm so over birthdays." And I thought of my mom who had just celebrated her 80th birthday with all the trimmings and even a life-sized Sesame Street Elmo character (was Elmo really just for the grandkids?) and began to smile at the memory. Lisa asked me what was so funny and I told her. I told her about the party and Elmo and that my mom didn't think she was too cool for anything. I said maybe that was why she's lasted so long. I ended by telling Lisa that she had no business being too cool for birthdays at 14 years of age.

Lisa's head swiveled to her right and she began biting her cheek. She looked up briefly to see if I was looking at her and accidentally caught my eye. She smiled in spite of herself, and instantly I softened to this isolated, doleful girl who so expertly kept people's affections for her at bay.

One workshop attendee of mine asked specifically about trying to work with kids who behave so disagreeably in session that they simply turn the therapist off. As long as the behavior is not so out of hand that the kid needs to be restrained, I responded, there are some options available to the therapist. A bad one is trying to modify the teen's behavior by setting up a system of consequences and rewards within the session: If the kid misbehaves, he loses a privilege. But what's going to be the privilege and reward for a teenager who doesn't want to be a part of the therapy in the first place? The whole thing becomes farcical and artificial. Anything that is happening by coercion is a therapy premised on control. It will not work.

Another option, not as contrived as the first but similarly useless, is to formally interpret the behavior as an expression of impersonal antipathy or resistance. This does nothing for the physically or verbally intimidating adolescent who already knows she's obstructing therapy. Of course she's obstructing it; she doesn't want it, no matter what reasons for her noncooperation are uncovered. No meaningful discussion of those reasons could ever come about without first the therapist's deep recognition of that client's wish *not* to be in therapy, said directly to the client. Many therapies with adolescents start to come apart at this juncture because the therapist tries too quickly to move the client past her resistance. They hope that by uncovering the reason behind the resistance, it will begin to dissolve. However, what happens is a shortchanging of the time needed to appreciate together with the client how very much she wishes to be somewhere other than in the therapist's office. Some therapists shortchange this period because they aren't sure what to say after their initial verbal acknowledgment (e.g., "I know it isn't your choice to be here," or "I know you've never felt that you've gotten anything out of therapy before and don't expect to now"), but "hanging a while" (half a session, maybe a couple of sessions) with that as the mutually recognized topic—*even if unspoken*—is more valuable than trying to eject it from the relationship between therapist and client, and the therapy.

Another option for working with a frankly disagreeable kid is for the therapist to comment on how the client's actions are affecting the way the therapist feels about him, and about working with him. This isn't done in a reprimanding or punitive way, nor in a patronizing, teasing, or imploring way. It's not even told in a manner that would have the adolescent think he's being told to knock it off. It can or cannot include a reference to why the therapist thinks the client is acting up, but it needs to be felt by the client as a personal revelation and not an academic pronouncement. In simple language, the therapist tells the adolescent that when he acts the ugly customer, the rowdy, the scamp, it just, well, changes things. Here are a couple of examples:

"I don't know what to do when you act up like that. I don't even know what I want to do, whether I want to stop the session or keep going or what. . . . But I do know that I don't want to sit here and take the hit."

"I keep trying to figure out why you go to all this trouble to try and rile me up, but I just come away from the whole thing with a sad feeling that it's all you know what to do with an adult you can't manipulate."

Therapists who get stuck believing that they have to protect their clients' feelings and manage the clients' discomfort more than their own in these situations are inevitably forced to tolerate indignities they wouldn't accept anywhere else in their lives. Rude is rude, whether it comes from a client, a neighbor, co-worker, or store clerk. It never helps an adolescent to let her ride roughshod over a therapist by calling him names, or threatening him, or destroying property in the office. It certainly doesn't earn the client his respect. The difficult task for the therapist is in deliberately addressing the interaction without offending the client's sensibilities in the process. Here's a sample exchange:

"Look, I don't want to have to play a guessing game of whether you will or won't follow through on your threats to smash up my pictures, so decide with me what we're going to do. Either I'll have to have your residential supervisor join us each session or we don't do this, but I can't be useful to you if I'm sitting here wondering each moment what you're going to do."

"If anyone else is in this room I won't tell you anything at all," the client replied.

"You don't tell me anything anyway. Besides, it's really your dilemma to figure out. I'm not interested enough in 'getting you to tell me things' that I'm willing to put up every time with your braggadocio. I'd really rather this be simple. You come. Maybe we talk. Maybe you get a new idea. I'm not interested in the fight."

Sometimes, no matter what a therapist tries, it becomes apparent that she simply isn't the right therapist for a particular client. And if she's thinking it, you can bet that the client is thinking it as well. Trying to hold out on addressing the issue directly, in the hope that a working alliance is right around the corner, is usually a mistake. So much more can be gained—and the therapy even saved—by a therapist's delicate candor in this precarious situation. An example follows:

"Beth, I don't know what it is but you and I don't seem to see eye to eye on anything. I don't think I've done anything in here yet to make you feel as if I have something valuable to offer, and I'm worried that you're convinced you're wasting your time with someone who simply can't help you. Maybe I can and maybe I can't, but what's more important is whether you think I can or not. Sometimes I feel that you're thinking you'd accomplish more with somebody else, a different therapist. And so here I am thinking all these things and I figure, well, why don't I just ask her about it? So I ask."

And Beth can look down and shrug or say, "No, it's okay here" or anything else and the therapist can nod and say, "Okay, well, we don't have to figure everything out today but I thought that as long as I was thinking all those thoughts I might as well ask you so I wouldn't be thinking them all by myself."

And a union might form, serendipitously, out of that simple interaction that spoke to the mutually experienced but previously unvoiced reality between them. Or not. And if not, then at least the client can appreciate the therapist's candor and wish *not* to pretend with her that something is happening that both know is not. That experience alone can be ther-

apeutic, even if subsequent conversations between the therapist and the adolescent go in the direction of making a
change in therapist. It's an experience to which the young
client mentally may frequently refer back, and an exposure to
genuineness that leaves a mark.

Benevolent candor allows a therapist to address other
sensitive things as well. Maybe the therapist believes she can
help the client but the client is doubtful because of differences in gender, race, sexuality, or ethnicity. This too is better handled openly, rather than trying to ride out the client's
unease and silent reservation without comment. Addressing
the issue draws on the therapist's finest communication skills
and tact, no doubt, but handled well, the ensuing discussion
can be a turning point in the therapy:

"Chris, there are things you say in here that lead me to
think you feel I can never understand you or the choices you
make. I worry sometimes that you're thinking that because
I'm white and you're Hispanic (you're gay and I'm not
gay/you've lived through harrowing life experiences that I
haven't/I'm someone of the opposite sex and three times your
age) I won't be able to understand or help you. Do you think
that?"

If Chris were to indicate that he did, then there appears a
wonderful opportunity to talk about his perceived limitations
of verbal communication to express one's inner life, memory,
personal experience, and sense of history, and connect to
another person. And that begs the question of whether he
would ever want to connect to another person whom he saw
as so different from him, and what it might mean to him if he
did: "Would you be surprised to find me understanding you?"
"Would it feel odd if you began to think of me as being helpful?" "Would it throw for a loop your thoughts about how people who are different from one another do or don't get
along?"

And if Chris were to have said initially that he didn't have any problem with the idea of a white therapist helping a Hispanic kid, then the therapist can say that's great, she'd just been wondering, she never knows for sure until she asks because some kids do feel funny about that sort of thing and so she wanted to bring it up. This underscores for the adolescent that it really is okay to talk about anything in that room, even the "unspeakable" topics, and that the therapist will make herself available to make that happen.

Using Candor and Sincerity to Confront

Communicating frankly helps make it easier to address sensitive issues with teenaged clients. It is also very useful when a therapist needs to directly confront a client's behavior or attitude in session. This was the only way in which I felt able to approach 17-year-old Tessa, who refused to acknowledge even my presence in the room with her. Tessa was brought for therapy by her mother, who was desperate to get Tessa to return to school, do some of her schoolwork, and stop screaming expletives at her all the time. Tessa was also very depressed, and, when in others' company, extremely sullen. She spoke to a couple of girls on her field hockey team and almost nobody else. Tessa had no interest in being seen for therapy, not because she denied needing help, but because she didn't believe therapy *could* help. The first session went nowhere with both Tessa and her mother present, so I decided to see Tessa alone for the second session. This was as nonproductive as the first session. She remained resolutely determined not to allow me to affect her in any way. I said, "You try so hard to avoid contact with me that it's no wonder you can't stand to come. It's too much work."

"I don't try to avoid contact with you," Tessa replied.

"Then tell me what you're doing when you don't look at me or talk to me."

Tessa shrugged, and I was again shut down. Hers was a different kind of silence, an aggressive one, designed not just to stop herself from talking but to stop the others as well.

"Have you always used your silence to shut people down?" (I didn't ask Tessa, *Do you always shut people down like this with your silence?* Phrased that way, it could come off as challenging, edgy.)

This got Tessa's interest, because she liked knowing she had an effect on people. She looked over at me and asked what I meant.

"Well, look, Tessa, I meet all the time with kids who don't want to talk in therapy. Even so, I usually get the sense that they're interested in my talking. So I talk, and eventually they join in. But with you, I get the sense that not only do you want nothing to do with me, you want me to have nothing to do with you, not even talking. I don't think you want me to say anything to you at all. Is this true?"

"Maybe," came her response.

I nodded and said, "Uh huh." I'd do more another time, but I liked stopping on a note of accord, no matter how tenuous. It was enough for now.

Another session came and Tessa allowed eye contact but no more. She told me her problems couldn't be solved with therapy and that we should stop meeting. I told her that it was for her and her mom to decide. Tessa's dad, living in another state and with whom I'd met once, had virtually no influence over his daughter.

"I think you should just see my mom, then. She's the one who thinks therapy can help."

"I did that already, Tessa," I answered, "during the first session when you walked out midway. You left us with plenty of time to talk."

Tessa looked away and smiled involuntarily.

I went on. "Nothing got accomplished because your mom needs you to be here, too. But when she is here, you just use it as an opportunity to shut her out as well. Last week she looked like she couldn't wait to get out of the room, and you looked relieved when she did."

Tessa smiled again, but this time didn't try to hide it from me. I decided to ask her about her style of affecting other people. I understood that Tessa liked to affect others in ways that made them uncomfortable. "I'm surprised you haven't asked me any questions by now."

"Why would I ask you anything?" Tessa replied.

"Not because you had any genuine interest, but because it would be an opportunity to prove your point—"

"What point?" asked Tessa, quickly.

"That anyone who makes apparent efforts to help you will invariably wind up feeling inept to do so."

Tessa ended up staring at me for a few moments before catching herself. She said nothing.

There are themes I was working here. One was Tessa's avoidance of interpersonal contact, presumably because she didn't want to destabilize her isolation. Another was her tendency to shut people down. A third was her message to everyone that she was not helpable, and that anyone who challenged this would be sorry they did.

Soon, in another session, I had an opportunity to use my self in my work with this sad and difficult girl. Tessa was telling me about the fights she and her mother had on an almost daily basis. The fights were calculated on her part, provocative and vile. I could tell that she wanted me to "intervene," but the invitation was not genuine. Had I bit the bait, she'd have shot down the idea dismissively. Tessa didn't want my advice; she wanted some sort of victory. When I didn't respond with the expected advice, Tessa got mad, and challenged my decision. "Aren't you going to say something helpful about our fights?"

"I wouldn't know what to say that would make a difference. I'm not even convinced you *want* me to say something helpful about the fighting. I half suspect you want me to say something so that you can tell me what a bad idea it is."

"Maybe I do."

I smiled.

"The truth is," Tessa added, "I really like to make my mom that mad. Besides, what would it matter to you anyway whether or not we fight or I call her a bitch all day long?"

"In the long run, Tessa, it won't matter to me. You're right. I just can't believe that it would never matter to you."

Tessa stared, bit her lip, and recrossed her legs. I was not saying that I didn't believe it didn't matter to her that she and her mother fought so violently, as if I knew something that she didn't. Instead, I was communicating to Tessa that I couldn't believe *anyone* wouldn't be affected by something like that over time. In other words, my comment to her had less to do with Tessa than with my conception of human relationships—that years of doing battle with one's mother would have to powerfully and negatively affect a person. I was not asking Tessa to do one thing differently; I was expressing my astonishment that she didn't want to.

I never was able to help Tessa and her mother, though. I couldn't find a way to move the sessions any further, and meeting with her parents didn't do the trick. I suggested, among other things, that they try working with someone else, who might prove to be a better match. I also thought that perhaps Tessa was too bound by her self-description as unhelpable to let therapy have any effect at all.

Four months later, however, Tessa's mom called again for help. Tessa was dangerously depressed and wanted to see me. Unfortunately, I had just had a death in my family, and wasn't seeing clients for several days. I sent them to an older, male colleague, and suggested they at least take care of the immediate crisis. But Tessa settled in with this new therapist, and has stayed on. I meet my colleague in the hallway from time to time, and he looks at me and says, "Boy, that Tessa . . ." I know I wasn't alone in finding it difficult to help her, but her story does underscore the need not to take a client's rejection of our assistance at immediate face value. Some people have more trouble than others in asking for what they know they need.

Chapter Six

Troubleshooting Individual Session Impasses

In spite of the most facile efforts on the part of a therapist, seasoned or not, there are invariably some moments when the therapy runs aground. Kids stop talking, stop coming, withdraw, or become antagonistic. Alternatively, they might be talking a blue streak but making no progress. The reasons for such shifts in the current are as numerous as there are personality and relationship variables; in addition, there are external influences on the working relationship, many unknown. Sandy's snarly, snappy fight with her well-meaning but overbearing parents that morning leaves her feeling scornful of all adults' efforts to help her straighten out her mixed-up life. Jay's feeling unjustly accused for antagonizing his younger brothers that afternoon provokes him to wear his anger on his sleeve all evening long, and his therapist bears the brunt of it during a 6 p.m. appointment.

Sometimes, a therapist who feels the session is in trouble reacts in ways to "save" it that serve only to exacerbate the problem. Angry, rebellious adolescents are very good at evoking within therapists the distinct and very unpleasant feeling that the therapy is out of control, or that the therapist is not adequately controlling the client or his participation in the session. These are things we don't have control over anyway. If a therapist acts in ways to suggest he believes he has this kind of control, he not only loses the battle for initiative in the therapy, but compromises his power to influence through his self; he has lost credibility. Therapists can allow themselves to be so committed to a kid's mental health that it's nearly palpable, but they should never want the client to change more than the client wants it himself. It's the difference between being compelling and being too urgent. The first engenders interest and, ideally, some kind of willingness to join the therapist. The second induces passivity and resentment, because

> Therapists spend years in graduate schools and hours in workshops learning how to join their clients, but few have successfully learned how to get their clients to want to join them.

it is too intrusive. Therapists spend years in graduate schools and hours in workshops learning how to join their clients, but few have successfully learned how to get their clients to want to join them. This is where we wind up trying too hard, or looking as if we care too much.

What follows are several of the more common scenarios that erupt during the darker days of a therapy, followed by suggestions for intervention.

✹

"Help! This Kid . . ."

". . . Won't Speak to Me"

Teenagers in therapy become uncommunicative for all kinds of reasons. Many are just so genuinely anxious that they really don't know what to say. Quite a few are wary about saying anything, for fear of being "analyzed," criticized, or patronized. Others are trying to keep a lid on their feelings, and think of therapy as the ultimate Pandora's box. Some don't like the therapist and want to maintain their distance, or are trying to one-up the therapist by exerting a control of silence over the encounter.

Others, like my client Nina, come into the therapy already feeling such a pressure to "predictably" produce material that they immediately resent the therapist's invitations to talk. Usually they develop this expectation after having been in therapies where there was a lot of pressure to talk about their problems. That had happened in Nina's case.

Nina was a rootin' tootin', sassy, and altogether likeable 16-year-old whom I saw for therapy at a residential center where she'd been sent by the state's children and youth services. Her background consisted of all the things you might expect of such a referral—emotional neglect, physical abuse, poor modeling for relationships, and the like—which had by now manifested in a provocative kid who eschewed school, bossed around the other girls on campus, and loved to tease the boys.

Nina wore her brazenness on her sleeve, and for my benefit shaped it into a rock-ribbed stance of silence for the duration of her sessions with me. She'd smile, drop a tidbit of information here and there, maybe tell an abbreviated tale or two, but there wasn't really much happening. I once wondered out loud to her why it seemed she and I had so much trouble keeping a conversation going when she was so delightfully chatty with her friends.

"Oh, I know what you're after," came Nina's reply.

"Huh?" came mine.

"I know what you're waiting to hear. All you therapists are alike."

"What am I waiting to hear?" I asked. I genuinely wondered.

"You're sitting there waiting for me to tell you all about my horrible childhood—how I was rejected and neglected, how I was abused, how I was suicidal and angry and everything! I know that's what you're waiting to hear."

"Wow," was my initial response, and then, "Boy, it just goes to show you don't need another person in order to have an argument. You can manage to argue with me all by yourself!"

Nina grinned and asked, "What do you mean?" She knew exactly what I meant but wanted to hear it anyway.

I thought of a story I once had heard from Dr. Robert Kravis. "You remind me of the story of a man whose car gets a flat tire. He has no tire jack, but spots a house a short distance away. He starts walking toward it, but begins wondering why anyone would be willing to loan him a jack since, after all, he was just a stranger on the side of the road. With no other choice, though, the man continues on. He stops in his tracks a few yards later to question once again why anyone would bother to loan him a jack. Having convinced himself that no one would, yet desperate for help, the man walks up to the front door of the house and knocks. A kindly gentleman answers the door and immediately asks if he could be of help, to which the man without a jack yells back, 'You can keep your stinking jack!'"

Nina loved this story, and laughed and laughed before looking straight into my face with what was her way of consenting to the work we wound up doing over the next 9 months. She knew that I both understood her and that I was not interested in hearing "scoop" about her apart from how it would serve her to tell me. I was neither voyeur nor archeologist, but instead just another adult who genuinely wanted to know how I might be of help.

What to Do

- Try getting the client to see that she is merely boxing shadows with her silence. So many of these clients come with expectations of therapists trying to draw them out; remaining silent is a way of stumping the therapist's intent. Help the adolescent realize that you have no interest in trying to *make* her talk, and if she chooses to remain silent all that will happen is—nothing. You won't fight back, so to speak, or make an adversarial issue of it, because it's always going to be more important that the client wants to speak than that the therapist is spoken to. If the client says, "Well, then how are you going to do any therapy if I don't tell you anything?" reply simply, kindly, and never facetiously that you don't know. If the teenager explains her silence by claiming to have nothing to say, some possible responses are:

Ask her where she thinks the two of you should go from there.

Ask if there's someone else in the family who would have stuff to say and should be invited.

Ask if there's something that the client would like *you* to say instead.

Ask if she thinks that if this wasn't a "therapy" session would she have more to say, and if so, how does the fact that this is a session change her ability to talk about things or herself.

Note that sometimes people have trouble getting started because it seems so artificial; then ask what could you or the two of you do to make it easier to get started.

To some adolescents who believe they're making a big point with me through their silence and unwillingness to join me at all, I'll tell them the story about a client who rallied for weeks with his silence, refusing ever to speak more than a few sentences to me over the course of a handful of sessions: "This kid marched all around campus [at the residential center where this took place] telling everyone how he won one over on Edgette," I describe. "He felt very proud of himself, but I am still wondering to this day how that felt so victorious to him. All I know is that he was such a lonely, unhappy kid, claiming such a lonely, hollow triumph." Then I shrug and change the subject so that the adolescent doesn't think I want him to respond.

This story is much more effective being heard than being discussed. Too much scrutiny strips it of meaning and impact. If the client wants to hear its message, he will. It's not the therapist's responsibility to *get* the silent client to talk any more than it is the therapist's fault if he doesn't. It *is*, however, the therapist's responsibility to be creative and nondefensive in helping that client *want* to talk.

> It is not the therapist's responsibility to get the silent client to talk any more than it is the therapist's fault if he doesn't. It is, however, the therapist's responsibility to be creative and nondefensive in helping that client want to talk.

- In a spirit of collaboration, invite the adolescent to help troubleshoot the silence with you. The gesture underscores the notion that (a) it isn't the therapist's job to get the teenager to speak but instead to create conditions in which the client wishes to speak, and (b) the solution will be found not in the therapist's unilateral management of the silence, but rather jointly.

An invitation like this could sound something like the following:

"Look, it's no secret that you and I are having a difficult time finding a way to get started. I want to make this easier for you but I'm not sure how to do that. Do you have any ideas how these sessions could go more smoothly?"

"I've been trying to figure out by myself how to get something going here, but I think I've been silly not to just ask you what you think. So, what do you think?"

The teenager may shrug, or look at you for a while without responding, or say he doesn't know. That's good enough for the time being; you were never really after or expecting an answer in the form of a concrete idea. You were just making an invitation.

- Give the adolescent permission not to talk. Most therapists are familiar with the paradoxical injunction of *prohibiting* talk, but I find that too clever. After all, I do want the client to talk with me, but not if it's forced. By giving the client *permission to withhold* from the therapist, the pressure to speak is relaxed. Moreover, in the climate of permissiveness, some of the appeal of withholding is lost. I find that handling the teenager's silence in this way demonstrates a measure of respect for the teenager's privacy that pays off in spades.

- When it is truly difficult to get anything started in an individual session, it's time to bring in the person who does have a complaint. This is usually a mom or a dad, but may be another relative or a staff member if the session is taking place at a school or residential center. They'll have lots to say, and you won't be sitting there wondering what you're supposed to be doing. Very rarely will I see a teenager alone anyway, and never for the first session, unless she is older (16 or 17), is not defying home or school rules, and is herself asking to be seen.

". . . Is Disrespectful in Session"

This is a familiar client. She's the one whose session you dread because it feels so darn . . . awful, awkward, long. This young client tries to intimidate the therapist through frank disrespect or by making contemptuous statements about what the therapist does for a living, as in the familiar "Hey, you're the therapist. Why don't you know?"

Get defensive here and you've entered a pit of quicksand. Adolescents who do this stuff love to get their therapists on the defensive, and there's little turning the discussion around once it starts to deteriorate. Kids who want to throw therapists off know that the best technique is to cut into their sense of being—or not being—helpful.

What to Do

- Deflect the comment so that it can't be taken personally, as the adolescent wishes it to be taken. Here's an example: Joey and his therapist are discussing Joey's tendency to get himself ejected from classrooms, scout meetings, karate class, and most recently, a friend's birthday party, because of a nasty mouth and nastier attitude. Joey sees this as happenstance, and accepts no responsibility for the repeated ejections.

"Joey," asks the therapist, in an ill-considered effort to illuminate his role, "why do you think that keeps happening to you all over the place?"

"I don't know. Don't *you* know?" Joey snorts. "You're the therapist here after all."

Bad response #1: "Yes, I am, but only you can tell us why people keep asking you to leave these places and situations." (The problem is that Joey doesn't *want* to tell you or himself. Why ask for something he doesn't want to deliver? You can only get "No" for an answer.)

Bad response #2: "What do you mean by that?" (Too defensive.)

Better response: "Of course I don't know. You haven't told me anything about yourself since we began meeting. How could I *possibly* know?"

• Without challenging him, point out to the client his role in the deteriorating session or conversation: "Are you going to keep asking me all those stupid therapist questions?" asks 14-year-old Sam, loud and brazen.

"Only if I keep having to try and get some kind of conversation going!" one could respond. "Frankly, I'd rather not. They're starting to sound stupid even to me. Spare us both and talk to me."

Passing handily on the invitation to be defined sarcastically as the expert, and responding without pretense or apology for what you couldn't have known in the first place, is one way to preempt a battle for control over who's *not* running the therapy.

- Collaboratively assess the motivation behind the teenager's remarks, without spouting interpretations that make it sound as if you know something that the kid doesn't:

    Bad comment #1: "Do you think you say things in here to try and upset me as your way of not letting me get to know you?"

    Bad comment #2: "Could it be that you're expressing anger toward me that you mean for other people, or for yourself?"

    Better comment: "You seem committed to throwing me off base, Taylor. Is there something about this that would please you?"

    Another possibility: "Why are you so intent on coming in here and antagonizing me, Maxine? I can't even take it personally because you don't even really know me! Help me understand what it is you want or are trying to say."

- Use empathy to diminish defensiveness on the adolescent's part. For example, "You know, honestly, I imagine this whole business does seem silly to you. They [the client's parents] want you to come, you don't. You're here, they're not. Maybe we need them here, too. What do you think?"

    One supervisee of mine worried that mentioning her client's displeasure with the therapy would make it a larger problem, somehow more real than before. Not to worry, I told her. It's like the business with suicide: Asking a kid if she is feeling like taking her life isn't going to create a problem that hadn't existed before. And addressing it directly will bring it to the fore where it can be more properly dealt with.

". . . Says He Doesn't Have a Problem"

No therapist worth her salt is really surprised when the adolescent client defers responsibility for the problems in her life. But what is surprising is how often a therapist considers her mission to correct this notion. Getting adolescents to admit that their problems are related to the choices they are making is not necessarily a therapeutic endeavor, especially if there is no sign of readiness on their part to consider this. It often can cause a kid to brace reactively against the therapist and turn off altogether to considering alternatives in action and attitude. Sometimes, the first part of therapy with reactive, acting-out teenagers involves helping the parents to articulate more clearly their expectations, set firmer limits, follow through with consequences for noncompliance, and hold the teenage accountable for his or her choices. Later on, maybe, and partly as a result of the parents imposing more structure, the teenager finds opportunities in session, or at home, to address problems more directly. It is critical that the parents be ready to hear the teenager at this juncture, and to be open and flexible in responding in ways that communicate a genuine desire to help their son or daughter find what he or she needs in order to make it easier to make better choices.

What to Do

Don't move forward on a session where you are already certain that you will be facing a kid, sitting by himself, who doesn't believe he has a problem or any use for the therapy. Bring in the person or people who *do* think the kid is in trouble, and let them speak. Whether or not the client gets involved is secondary as long as the other parties are in positions to either influence him or impose consequences for inappropriate behavior or noncompliance with responsibilities. Spending time soliciting the teenagers interest is nonproductive, and makes it less likely that he'll find a way to plug into the therapy later on. Keep the therapy moving with the people who are playing and the teenager will find his own way to join in.

Problems that are less measurable than inappropriate or noncompliant behavior, however, may be harder to address without the adolescent's cooperation. The middle-school boy of divorcing parents who hides his depression behind a wall of video games needs someone to kindly challenge his denial without forcing himself on the boy. It's the same with the high school senior who has become debilitated with anxiety about her future. These kids and others like them may say they don't need help, that they're all right, that their depression or anxiety or pessimism or need for control is no big deal. Having their parents initially carry the family sessions by talking about why they are worried about their child is one way to help this adolescent—without ever directly imposing on the nonparticipating teenager to join in the conversation, the parents and therapist can help explain, contextualize, and sympathize with the teenager's emotional condition in a way that he can draw vicarious benefit.

Sometimes, however, the therapy has to wait for a better time. Fifteen-year-old Caren was brought in to see me at her own request. I'd seen the family for much of the past year regarding Caren's brother's chronic school refusal, academic failure, and belligerent attitude within the home. The parents had been divorced for several years, and neither Caren nor her brother enjoyed the company of their tempestuous and overcontrolling father.

Caren complained of feeling depressed for quite some time, years maybe, she didn't know. She felt burdened by friends who came to her for guidance and support for their problems. She had no hobbies, and did the smallest amount of physical activity she could get away with. She didn't read. She had no favorite music artist.

It turned out that Caren didn't want the help as much as she wanted to know that her therapist (me), her psychiatrist (to whom I had referred for medication evaluation), her school counselor, and her mom would be available for her. She wanted them at her behest, but she had no intention of using them. Time after time, Caren asked her mom to schedule an appointment with me, only to refuse to go at the last minute or decline conversation once in session. She would lay back on the couch and shrug her answers to my questions, grow annoyed with her mother's admonitions to participate, and gradually recede more and more into the background. Caren would become sarcastic, or play dumb with me. She didn't want therapy; she only wanted to know that she could get it were she to ask. She did the same thing with us all.

In Caren's presence, I said to her mom that I thought it more important to her daughter that people respond to her need for support when asked to than that she take advantage of it. Although I knew Caren didn't want to feel depressed, I believed she found that easier to tolerate than accepting the help available to and orchestrated by her. Caren was very counterdependent, and I thought this was what accounted for her being both the one to whom all her friends gravitated to with problems and the one who experienced enormous discomfort accepting the very solace and support she unrelentingly doled out.

I suggested to Caren and her mom that we hold off on sessions for a while and speak in a few weeks' time. I told Caren that I thought it was difficult for her to accept help from all of us therapists and counselors trying to lift her out of her depression. I also warned that sometimes depression can make you think funny things, untrue things—like *No one would want to help me anyway. They're all just faking it to be nice*, or *I'm not really worth being helped*, or *I couldn't be helped even if they tried*—and that she should be on the lookout in case she ever started to have thoughts like those. My door would remain open, I told Caren and her mom, and I encouraged them to call me with an update in a couple of weeks. In the meantime I'd moniter Caren through her mom and her school counselor, who was following her as well.

Family therapy would have been the most obvious other option; I suspected a considerable part of Caren's depression was related to her volatile and near-estranged relationship with her dad. But Caren refused any part of this, and I knew her mother would not be capable of getting her to a session if her father was present. The father probably would have brought her by force, exacerbating the control battles in their ravaged relationship. No thanks. All in all it wasn't my preferred outcome, but it was a way to position Caren so that she could sit back or move forward and still get the support she wanted at a pace that worked for her.

I haven't seen Caren for a couple of months now but keep in touch with her mom by telephone. Caren is doing okay, her mom tells me. She's a little more active with her friends, and a little less sad-looking around the house. Caren knows she's welcome to schedule a session anytime. While hoping that Caren becomes better emotionally and socially adjusted in the coming years, Caren's mom feels the situation now to be less urgent. Caren no longer talks about feeling so depressed, and seems to be making good decisions in her personal life. Her schoolwork remains satisfactory, and her relationship with her mother, at least, very good. Sadly, she continues to refuse to work on her relationship with her father. My plan at this point is to follow up again at the beginning of the next school year, and see if and where there might be some plasticity in family situation through which some change can be promoted.

". . . Says She Doesn't Trust Me"

A classic ploy. Cagey teenagers paired up with therapists who want too much to help find it easy to tempt them into "proving" they are worthy of confidences. But, alas, nothing is ever quite convincing enough, and so the kid demurs further, and the therapist tries harder to demonstrate trustworthiness. The best way out of this mess that I know of is not allowing the therapy to be defined as needing trust in order to work. Trust is a relative and slippery concept anyway—someone trusts or doesn't trust a therapist to do what? To say what? Is a therapist who keeps secrets but uses poor judgment better than one who will only hear things with the whole family present? What is more important to trust—a therapist's competence, his discretion, his benevolence, or his conceptualization of problems? In the absence of context and detail, the concept becomes meaningless, a gratuitous "gift" from client to therapist that probably has little bearing on an adolescent's real feelings about whether or not that therapist is competent to help her.

What to Do

- Redefine therapy as a process that functions on a variety of premises, some involving trust and some not. You can meet claims of adolescent clients that they aren't sure they trust you with: "Tell me, what does that have to do with you and I having a conversation?"

"Well, how can I talk to you if I don't know whether I can trust you or not?"

"Don't know. You'll have to figure out what you're comfortable telling me and what you're not. If it would help, you can tell me what you feel you need to know that would make a difference."

If the adolescent is legitimate in his concerns, he'll ask a legitimate question, for example, "How do I know you won't go discussing with my parents stuff that I tell you about?"

"You don't. You don't because I don't, until I know what it is we would be talking about. If you're in danger, or involved in doing something that your parents would feel they have a right to know about, I would feel wrong sitting here with that kind of secret. It's not mine to keep. If stuff comes up that's personal and doesn't need to involve others, or there's a problem but we're able to manage it safely and quickly here, that's a different story. What you'll need to trust, Billy, is not whether I'm going to keep your confidences, but my judgment to handle in your best interests all the stuff that could come up."

- Don't allow the client to turn talking in therapy into a quid pro quo. "How come I'm supposed to tell you all about me and you don't have to say anything about yourself?"

"You don't have to tell me anything, Bonnie. If you want to, great, and if not, I'll suppose you have your reasons."

"What about you? How come you don't say anything?"

Bad response #1: "Because therapists aren't supposed to talk about themselves. This is really about you, and for you." (Too patronizing, and very ungenerous of the therapist.)

Bad response #2: "I get the sense that you don't want to tell me anything about yourself unless I've told you something about myself. Why do you think it's important for you to know about me first?" (Talk about putting the kabash on a conversation! Why push reluctant, teenaged therapy clients to answer a question like that? Besides, the answer is pretty obvious—they're buying time, or trying to figure the therapist out, or feel very self-conscious of having to reveal themselves unilaterally. Can you blame them? What's to understand?)

Better response #1: "What is it you'd like me *to* say, Bonnie? I'd be happy to say a lot of things in here. I just don't know what they are yet, until we get talking."

Better response #2: "I *do* end up talking about myself with my clients, Bonnie. I tell them what I think, what I feel, sometimes what I do. But it happens when neither one of us is looking for it to happen or not happen. It just comes out of some conversation we've been having."

Better response #3: "Bonnie, if I really believed that your comfort talking to me depended on your knowing a certain fact or figure about me, I'd probably tell you what you wanted to know in a minute. What I believe instead is that this is an awkward situation for you, and one that you didn't arrange for yourself. I can only imagine that you're thinking *There's no way I'm going to sit here and spill my guts to this lady while she just listens and stares back.* Well, I can't promise a lot of things in here but I can promise that I won't leave you stuck doing all the talking. And I won't stare."

- Avoid promising something you cannot deliver. One of my supervisees recently asked me for help in managing the case of a 16-year-old boy who had confided in session that he was smoking marijuana—not just the occasional time his parents believed—but every day. Gerry wondered what to do. He thought the pot smoking had become more than he and the boy could get a handle on in session, but the client had assumed a confidentiality.

    "From whom?" I asked Gerry. Well, largely from him, it turned out. Gerry had mistakenly promised the boy that anything they discussed in session would stay between them. He never should have promised this. I've known instances in which a therapist will offer confidentiality as a way to convince the client to talk, and maybe that had happened here. But what really gets communicated to the client is that it is more important to the therapist that the client talk than it is to the client, so important that the therapist will offer what is tantamount to a bribe. What happens as a result is that he loses credibility, and quite possibly gets stuck, like Gerry did, having to go back on his word because his promise conflicted with his ethical need to inform parents of behavior that he saw as growing increasingly out of hand.

". . . Tries to Pick a Fight"

I once worked with a girl I started calling my "Oh boy" case. Every time I looked in my appointment book to see who I had for the day and saw her name, I'd say to myself, "Oh boy."

Violet, 16, was one of the coyest and most difficult adolescent clients with whom I'd ever worked. I was her seventh or eighth therapist in as many months, and she enjoyed playing us like fiddles. It was more important to Violet that she made everyone around her more uncomfortable than she was, and keep them at bay, than to get the help she knew she desperately needed.

Violet had been referred to me by her attending psychiatrist at the hospital where, the previous week, she'd been stabilized for anorexia nervosa and depression. She'd been hospitalized several times before, and the staff were familiar with her provocations and attempts at manipulation. When her psychiatrist told Violet that she was being discharged, Violet threatened immediate suicide. The psychiatrist replied, "Well, then you'll be dead." And with that, Violet was sent to my office.

Thanks a lot.

Violet's first comment was that she'd been sent to me because none of her other therapists would take her back. She waited for me to ask her why, so she could tell me how bad she was. I didn't ask. She wanted to know how much my sessions cost (I told her) and whether I was worth that fee (I told her that I thought so but that she might feel differently). Had I ever lost a client to suicide? No. Did I know she was suicidal? I had heard that she said she was going to commit suicide if she were discharged. Did I really think I could help her? I had no idea yet, I responded.

"Do you want to work with me?" Violet asked.

"I think so," I replied.

"Why?" Violet wondered.

"I'm not sure," I answered honestly.

Violet softened after this interchange, and began telling me about herself. She loved being a subject of conversation, and was very forthright about her problems. She never, how-ever, took seriously the job of solving them. Violet was needy, attention seeking, and able to use her wit to retain the atten-tion even of people she had just alienated. I supposed that was part of why I was still interested in helping her after that opening interrogation. She was a compelling character in spite of herself.

Violet tried mightily and unrelentingly to start conflicts with me or frictions of some sort, any sort. Having become weary of dodging her efforts to get something started, I finally remarked that she seemed pretty determined to get us on opposite sides of the fence. I told her that she needn't try so hard as sooner or later there probably would be something I'd say or do in session or neglect to say or do that would gen-uinely render her unhappy with me. But that didn't worry me, I told her. What did worry me was how we were going to man-age to come through the other end of it, because every other time she'd gotten angry with her therapist she blew the ther-apy out of the water.

I continued. "Violet, look, one day I'm going to ask you a question and you're going to hate it. Or you'll ask me a ques-tion and not like my answer. That part's okay. What's impor-tant, though, is that we can keep talking with one another in spite of things we feel differently about. And the reason I bring it up is that you've told me every time you've gotten mad at your therapist you decide not to go anymore. I don't want that to happen here."

What To Do

- A strategy of *forecasting the inevitable*, and trou-bleshooting for it together in advance, is a handy way of defusing anticipated frictions between therapist and client. It accomplishes a number of things:

1. Forecasting takes the edge off of any conflict because, after all, the conflict has been predicted. Anything that's been predicted is less intimidating once it arrives on the scene. Also, when some form of conflict has been defined as predictable, it becomes an expected part of the therapy process rather than an indication that things have come undone or are spinning out of control. Predicting a problem is only necessary, however, for clients with whom some form of conflict is seemingly unavoidable.

    A strategy of forecasting the inevitable, and troubleshooting for it together in advance, is a handy way of defusing anticipated frictions between therapist and client.

2. Forecasting serves as a stabilizing reference point in the middle of what might have otherwise become an awkward point in a session. The therapist can reference back to "that day when we spoke about this happening in here. What did we say about how we were going to handle this situation?" It suddenly focuses the adolescent's attention on solving the problem, and reminds him that this is something that was expected to occur at some point, and had been prepared for. Some examples include:

    •   The therapist can say to the client, "Hey, Owen, remember we thought something like this might happen. The point to remember is that we both want the same thing here—you and your folks getting along, and you enjoying your free time better. I'm on your side."

- The therapist can remind the client about an earlier conversation they had had concerning people's differing comfort levels with conflict: "I know this feels to you like an end-of-the-road discussion, but think back to our last conversation about this. Whenever you feel that you and another person are the slightest bit out of step, you're ready to toss in the towel. This is not a deal-breaking conversation we're having. Let me help you learn to disagree with someone and still keep the relationship intact."

3. Forecasting a problem with a client allows it to be later *externalized* from both therapist and client,* and be experienced as something they face together rather than as something that stands between them.

- Relabeling or interpreting an adolecent's challenging attitude as something more than wanting to provoke has its therapeutic value, but requires timely and sensitive expression in order to avoid patronizing the adolescent. Unless credence and respect is afforded to whatever the client is expressing, relabeling can come off as something that the therapist knows better about the teenager than the teen herself, as in, "Oh, you're not really angry with me, you're just feeling defensive/vulnerable/insecure because . . ." That

---

*White, M. (1989, Summer). The externalizing of the problem and the re-authoring of lives and relationships. *Dulwich Center Newsletter,* 3–21; White, M., & Epston, D. (1990). *Narrative means to therapeutic ends.* New York: Norton.

is therapy adolescents dislike. A therapist might get a better response saying to a client, "Sometimes when you try so hard to drive your point home I get the feeling you're worried that I won't ever hear you unless it's banged into my head. Don't worry, Carly, I hear you. I make it a point to listen to everything you are saying."

- Reframing the behavior or attitude goes beyond giving it a different name—it extends to imbuing the act with different meaning. Reframing, in Violet's case, could have involved describing her behavior as something she did to protect herself against difficult feelings/loss of control/vulnerability, and a cue to slow the therapy down. Again, the therapist needs to be careful that this doesn't come off as a patronization and dismissal of the teen's anger.

So many especially challenging teenaged clients use their time in therapy to try and agitate a therapist in order to maintain a sense of control over the process of therapeutic interaction. Their thinking is that whoever can make the other feel more is more in control of the interaction. Adults do this all the time with each other in a series of never-ending relationship power plays: man makes the woman sad, woman makes the man angry, he makes her sadder, she makes him angrier. The kid who is so busy evoking reactions from his therapist and the other adults in his life never has time to become aware of what he himself is feeling. I might just say that to a client who was relating this way. I wouldn't say that he needed to stop doing what he was doing—only that I understood it, could explain more if he wanted to hear more, and was going to decline reacting in kind. I would explain what I thought he lost by interacting in that way, and help him to see how I might be limited in helping him if he continued. Time and again I find this to be a very effective way to interest an adolescent client in how he affects other people.

". . . Talks About Everyone Else in the World but Herself"

This kid tells you all about the adventures and escapades of her friends. She tells you nothing about herself.

What to Do

- Avoid interpreting this as a way for the teen to avoid talking about her own problems. She already knows that, and telling her so is useless.

- Instead, ask her what winds up happening to those other kids in their escapades. Show an interest in the client's perceptions of what does or doesn't happen. Make interesting observations yourself without lecturing: "She acts as though her shenanigans won't ever catch up with her!" or "He seems to love to get into people's faces, doesn't he!?" This allows the adolescent to see how you will react when she begins finally to tell you about her escapades.

- If the teenager doesn't start personalizing his stories within a couple of sessions, go ahead and express directly what you're thinking. Some examples are:

  "You know, I'd love to help you with the problems going on at home, but I don't know how to since we only talk about your sister!"

  "By the time we're done working together I'll have been able to help everyone else in your school but you. How can we get this conversation turned around so that I can be useful to you instead?"

"It's so hard for you to talk to me about you. . . . How can I make it easier?"

". . . Just Keeps Complaining About Everyone Else"

The adolescent client who comes into session and only complains about what everybody else is doing to foil his plans to lead the good life can be trying. No amount of "logic" is going to convince him that the best thing he can do for himself is to assume more responsibility for his life and stop complaining.

What to Do

Rather than assume the burden of convincing her of that, try instead to pose questions or assume therapeutic positions that cause her to come to those conclusions herself. Examples include:

- "That sounds pretty awful. You talk as if you're hoping I can change your parents' minds about that. Are you?"

    If the answer comes back "Yes," respond with "I have no idea how I'd convince them to do it any differently and I'm not certain that I would."

    "You mean you think a 10:00 curfew is right for me? I'm 16!"

    "It may be, it may not. I don't know. That's their decision. Tell me what got them so angry last weekend that they scaled it back and maybe I can help you to regain your privilege."

- Another response could be: "I have no doubt that all those ridiculous things are happening at school, Tamara, but what is it that we can do in here that could make a difference for you?"

  "Nothing."

  "Well, then, we're really stuck because I have no influence over that group of girls at lunch. Maybe I have influence over you. I'm never sure." (smile)

- Or consider this: "It makes no difference whose fault it is or who was right or wrong. The deal is that you are in deep doo doo at school and unless you figure a way out of the mess you'll wind up sacrificing the whole year. Then you can be as right as you want to be—all through summer school."

- Another tactic is: "Look, it's no secret to us that you don't ever like to see yourself as being part of the problem, but until you figure out some of your contribution to that situation and do something about it I worry you'll be singing this tune three months from now and still be just as miserable."

This reminds me of a 15-year-old boy I'd been working with at a residential treatment center. Neal constantly complained about how all the adults in his life pried too much into his business:

"My teachers keep bugging me all the time for assignments!"

"My parents want to see me jump through all these hoops just to be able to go out for a night."

"Even you keep asking me all these dumb questions that you want me to answer."

"Neal," I said to him one day, "you act as if you weren't in control of any of these things. Get your assignments in and obviously your teachers will go after someone else who's blowing off his homework. And of course your parents want you to clean your room and take out the trash before you go out. Can you blame them? They don't want to get stuck with your chores while you trot through the mall with your buddies. As for me, I'll stop asking all these dumb questions as soon as I feel I don't have to use them to jumpstart our conversations. I get sick of hearing them myself! How sad that the ball has been in your court all this time and you didn't even recognize it."

". . . Plays Coy"

"I've got a secret that you want to know and I don't know if or when I'm going to tell you." This is the sometimes spoken and sometimes unspoken message from the adolescent who uses her "material" to play cat and mouse with the therapist. However, it only works if the therapist is dying to know what the secret is. She doesn't. She's more interested in why the client wants to play with her like that.

What to Do

Ask the client why he prefers to work so hard to get you to ask him something he wants you to know.

- "Corey, you tell me all these stories and hint that there's more to them than you're sharing. I always feel like you want to tell me but won't unless I ask first. If I don't ask, you don't tell, even though you want to! How does that work?"

- "Laurie, I can tell by now that you have something you've been wanting me to ask you about, and all I'm wondering is why you wouldn't just tell me what it is. I'll ask you, because I know you really want me to. But maybe afterward, you'll tell me why that way seems better to you than telling me yourself."

Responding obligingly but with comment to a client's need to handle things in what appear to be convoluted ways is an alternative to asking the adolescent to explain her coyness outright.

". . .Tries to Regale Me With His Tales of (Mis)Adventure"

"Watch my exciting life but don't try to make me change it in any way!" is what this adolescent communicates. The task here for the therapist is managing to constructively balance the fine line between not taking the bait of "intervening" when he knows that the help will be rejected, and not condoning the antics through silence.

What to Do

- Comment on the effect that the adolescent's actions are having on the session or on you, not their purpose. "We get so busy in here hearing about your escapades that we never have time to talk about anything else. Like whether or not they're such good things for you to be doing. They actually sound like such lonely stories to me, Ray."
- Comment on the dilemma the adolescent's style puts you in, and what you think would happen were you to

act as you wished to. "Jeri, what am I supposed to do with this story? If I say you're getting yourself into trouble, you'll scoff at me and turn away. Then you'll punish me by refusing to talk to me for a session or two. If I just listen without responding, I feel like an idiot because I'm not saying what I think. I'm not sure what to do here."

• Wait patiently.

I had a client, 19 years of age. Audrey was very guarded, defensive, sarcastic, demure, and intelligent. In the months following her serious suicide attempt and subsequent hospitalization, she revealed to me in her original twice-a-week and eventual once-a-week sessions only bits and pieces about herself. Yet everything about her indicated that this was the only pace she could tolerate, and that she wanted to continue meeting. Eventually her bits and pieces gave way to stories about her drinking with friends. Drinking a lot. And smoking pot. And having casual sex with different partners. But all stories were "hands off." Audrey never said as much, but I sure knew as much. They were *her* stories, and she revealed them carefully, as if they were precious jewels. I was not to touch.

Audrey was different from the kind of youngster I described earlier in this section. She wasn't trying to entertain, impress, or shock me with her stories, and she didn't want me to react. She wanted me to hear her stories and *not* react. She wanted to tell me about herself, and her weekend warrior stories were the only way she knew how to accomplish that. It was a test of sorts, of a good and understandable kind, to see if I could pick up on her unvoiced cues, respect her parameters of disclosure, and still want to help her unconditionally. I think she also was testing herself to see if she could let me hear her tales and still come back in the next week and look me in the eyes. I passed her test, and she passed her test. Audrey told me more and more each week as I said less and less.

Eventually I noticed Audrey waiting for me to respond. She was giving me "permission" to intervene with her, and I treated it respectfully. I kept my comments easy, nondirective, and sparing. It was another few months before I discovered that Audrey was going out less and spending more time with her college studies. She had also reduced her drinking markedly. I found this out by listening to the changes in her stories (reducing work hours so she could study more, turning up regularly as the designated driver for her friends) and not through Audrey's telling me—it was never her style to be so direct. Audrey reminded me a lot of Helen, the dignified and private 15-year-old I discussed in Chapter 2, who knew exactly how to get her life back in order once she chose to do so, and who needed only my support and not my direct guidance. Some kids (typically older, a little self-controlling, and above average in intelligence) work better that way, and they tell us early on in the therapy which ones they are.

". . . Storms Out of the Room and Won't Come Back"

These are awkward, volatile situations that easily cause a therapist to try too hard to "fix" the session in ways that are countertherapeutic. The therapist may try to talk an angry, threatening adolescent out of leaving by offering to temporarily change the subject or stop talking himself. He may try to explain his comments in a way that comes off as defensive or unconfident. Or the therapist might be tempted to follow the adolescent outside the office and hold the remainder of the session in a parking lot or fast-food restaurant where it is believed the teenager feels more "comfortable." But the teenager has to learn to be comfortable (enough) in the therapist's office for therapy to work. Accommodating the teenager's anger, frustration, or low tolerance for self-examination by "softening" the discussion or modifying the setting is costly to the therapy, and does little to help the client learn to temper her reactiveness. A therapist can continue to present himself as very supportive to the adolescent and sympathetic to her need to react extravagantly without needing to track the client's attempts at avoidance.

When an adolescent in a family session storms out and it's thought that she is in danger of doing something she shouldn't, a parent goes out to find her and supervise. Perhaps she decides to come back to the session, but if not, the session continues with the remaining parent. If the adolescent stormed out to have a hissy fit and is not believed to be a safety risk, then she is left alone to do what she needs to but the session continues with the parents. The adolescent's leaving should never be allowed to be a show stopper, unless there is some urgent safety matter at hand. A most unproductive approach would be to try and talk the client into returning. If she's standing around obviously waiting to be asked, however, a therapist might offer a face-saving invitation such as, "Are you done with us for the day, or did you want to join us again?"

An adolescent's leaving should never be allowed to be a show stopper, unless there is some urgent safety matter at hand.

If such a session continues with only the parents present, they should be advised not to discuss the rest of the session with their child afterward. If he wants to know what was discussed, they should tell him that he can find out at the next session. That next session should be treated as business as usual, but if the adolescent refuses to go, the parents should

attend and either work with the therapist to discourage the
teen's refusal through setting up some consequences, or
reconfigure the therapy (perhaps doing parent sessions only)
to work in spite of the adolescent's nonparticipation.

Aaron stormed out and refused to attend family sessions
once his parents started challenging his belligerent attitude
more strongly. He had had a good run for a while, storming
around the house, slamming doors, leaving dirty dishes
everywhere, blowing off chores. When his parents began
holding him more accountable for his actions and decisions,
he blew off therapy. I told Aaron's parents that attending sessions should be considered part of his job, like going to
school or helping his dad with the family's lawn business on
Saturdays, and that if he didn't attend (he needed only to
come—whether or not he chose to speak was up to him) they
should impose consequences similar to those he incurred if
he skipped school or work. No drama, no showdowns, I
encouraged them—just the consequences of no going out, or
no car privileges, or no friends over for that week.

One week of seeing his parents mean business was
enough for Aaron. He sulked back into sessions and wound
up having a lot to say about his parents' contradicting and
mercurial parenting styles, which had been driving him batty,
as it turned out, and inciting him to tune them out.

What to Do

- If there are no parents around, then certainly it's the
  therapist's responsibility to locate the teen—to make
  sure that she is under control, not necessarily to continue the session—unless the teen chooses to continue it. To help the teen make that choice, the

therapist can offer a question like "Do you think we can manage to go on from here?" If the session does continue, the therapist can try exploring with the client what happened, but must focus on what happened *between the therapist and client* and not just on what happened *within* the adolescent, which can make her feel defensive or angry all over again. If the adolescent volunteers a more introspective explanation, that's fine, but those who storm out of rooms are unlikely to be the kind of client who can do that. Asking a client "What happened between us (or between you and your parents) just then that made you need to leave so abruptly?" reveals a therapist's willingness to be part of the process rather than only a clinical observer, and is a more collaborative way to look at the blowup than "What got you so upset?"

- The therapist can also help the kid out with his own thoughts on what happened instead of leaving it up to the client to explain. For example: "I knew you were going to walk out as soon as I opened my mouth, but if I don't speak up I feel that I'm being held hostage to your temper. My choices are to bite my tongue so you'll stay in the room, but then I'm as good as useless, or talk to you and assume the risk of you walking out. They're lousy options. Can we figure something else out?"

- Sensitively defusing the adolescent's anger and preempting her need to leave the session is possible by relating with her in the moment in very straightforward ways: "I don't mind you being so mad in here, but what are you doing being so mad at me?! Tell me so that maybe I can be mad *with* you!"

Where a therapist could lose a kid here is by saying things like:

"Why are you getting so angry?"

"Calm down so we can talk about it rationally."

"What thoughts are you having right now?"

- Another more candid and straightforward attempt to stay connected to the upset adolescent is as follows:

"It sure feels like I just became the enemy in here! What happened, Caitlin?"

"Malcolm, I can't figure out what exactly I'm not understanding yet. Give me some more help before you blow me off."

". . . Says That I Don't Understand What She's Going Through"

You may not. But why does she think that she can't describe her situation well enough so that you *can* understand?

What to Do

I'd ask why she has so little faith in her words to communicate that, or in herself. If the adolescent suggests that she's done a fine job of articulating her situation but you still don't understand, then ask, without sounding defensive, where she thinks you're missing the boat. Help her to help you, and consider seriously that you may really not be comprehending the client for personal reasons (e.g., you're not flexible enough in perspective, you're too defensive, there's countertransference, etc.).

". . . Just Keeps Telling Me That He Could Change Things Around Any Time He Wanted To"

What to Do

- You smile and say, "That's great." You don't challenge him to prove it. You don't ask why, then, hasn't he done that. You don't ask when he's going to make those changes. You just smile and ask if he thought he might ever want to do something like that. If he shrugs and says that he sometimes thinks so, you easily ask how he typically makes decisions like that. And then you wait.

   If you pounce on what the teenager is saying and take it at face value, you're likely to get one of any number of miserable interactions, such as the following: The therapist says, "You keep telling me you could change things around any time you wanted to, so why haven't you done it?" (He hasn't done it because he doesn't want to. His therapist and mom and dad and teacher want him to. He doesn't.)

   The client responds, "Haven't really thought about it."

   "When do you think you'll start thinking about it?"

   "Whenever."

   The misassumption here is that the client and the therapist have similar agendas. They probably don't.

- How else can this go? The therapist could say, "So what do you think we ought to do in the meantime?"

   "What do you mean?"

   "I mean, until you feel like changing anything. What should we do in the meantime?"

   The teen is puzzled. "I don't know."

The lack of pressing, the curious complacency with the adolescent's timeline for change, and the question about what else to do result in a momentary softening in the client, as evidenced by his response. There is no need to do more at this moment; the therapy was the communication of the therapist's respect for what the client said. It says a lot, and does a lot. Later, when the time is right, the therapist uses the client's confidence in her to begin pressing about changing things around.

Chapter Seven

Orchestrating Productive Family Sessions With Challenging Adolescents

P roblems that can be a death song for a therapist meeting alone with a reluctant teenaged client are much more easily managed when you have the client's family in the room with you. Having other people involved in the sessions also keeps the adolescent's lack of participation from halting the work. But not all kids come with a family, and some have families whose members won't or can't show up, or who are not real resources because of their own problems. That's why prior chapters discussed clinical situations that happen in both individual and family therapies. These next two chapters, however, describe a family model of intervening with adolescents who have significant behavioral and emotional problems. Chapters 7 and 8 focus on many of the same principles as earlier chapters—preserving the dignity of the adolescent client, relating with genuineness and candor, holding the adolescent accountable for what he is choosing to do or not to do—but they add the element of aggressively helping the parents to help their teenager during and in between sessions, as well as after the therapy has concluded.

Problems
that can be a death
song for a therapist
meeting alone with a
reluctant teenaged client are
much more easily managed
when you have the client's
family in the room
with you.

✳

Preventing Problems in the First Place

Get the Parents in From the Beginning

It does no good for a therapist to sit in front of a reluctant teenager and try to discuss the teenager's problems. It does worse than that, actually, because it sets the therapy up to be one where the therapist appeals repeatedly to the teenager for her involvement. Most unwilling teenage clients simply communicate with "Uh, no, I don't think so."

Because it's the parents' idea that the teenager be in therapy, the parents need to be in the office with their child to tell the therapist what matters are concerning them (the therapist won't hear this from the adolescent himself), and this needs to happen in front of the adolescent. If the parents come in alone beforehand and tell you everything, it terribly limits the next session when the parents and adolescent come in together. You have already heard all the issues, so the session can only start poorly, by either (a) the therapist relaying what he's heard from the parents—a lousy stance in which the therapist has now formally aligned with parents and comes off paternalistically; (b) the parents tell it all again for the kid's benefit, but both he and the therapist have already heard it all, so it's old news (a dull, flat, going-nowhere session); or (c) the parents and therapist ask the adolescent what the matter is, to which he responds, "Don't you guys already know? You're the ones who set up the appointment" or "There's no problem. My parents are the ones with a problem. Go ask them."

Exceptions to the Rule

As with all rules, sometimes there are circumstances under which the parents and teen should not meet together. These can include:

- The situation with the teenager is so out of control and volatile that no productive conversation can take place with the teenager in the session; in this case the therapy, to start, is probably going to revolve mainly around the parents, with them making the changes in management that bring about a difference. In such cases, the first few sessions may be with the parents alone, for the purpose of helping them strategize management, helping them enforce it, or getting them to other referrals such as a consultation for medication. The teenager joins the session once she is able to be part of a conversation and can stay reasonably civilized in the face of the inevitable controversy and disagreement that will erupt.

• The teenager is being seen at a residential treatment center or some other venue in which the parents are unavailable. In this circumstance, the therapist takes the position of, "Look, this is what your residential supervisor and teachers say are problems. I don't know if you find that to be the case, too. That's what concerns them. What concerns you?" This way, the adolescent knows what you know, but sees that you aren't another do-gooder agent of the staff.

• The parents are psychologically unavailable to help their child, or there has been such a strong history of neglect or abuse that it is inappropriate for the early therapeutic work to be done with everyone together.

• A parent is so volatile or berating toward the adolescent that it is not productive to work with them together.

• A mature 16- or 17-year-old asks for therapy himself, for problems he feels he can (and wants to) address himself, and the parents are supportive of this.

• Some very effective individual therapies grow out of a successful course of family therapy that has enabled the adolescent to subsequently take advantage of therapy on her own.

Open the Session by First Addressing the Parents

A first family session generally has the therapist sitting in front of a cluster of related people who are having trouble getting along. The parents look at the therapist and the adolescent doesn't. They are all waiting for the therapist to speak.

Avoid starting with the teenager. He didn't request the meeting. Start with the parents, or with an open question directed to anyone/everyone. See who speaks and go from there.

Do Not Take the Parents' Conceptualization of the Problem(s) at Face Value

Scan for all possibilities, even if the family is resolute in their conceptualization and presentation of the problem. Buying in to their assessment without developing your own independent judgment closes the lens prematurely and robs everyone of your expertise. Also bear in mind that families with teenagers who have been causing problems for some time tend to get overly focused on the problem and lose perspective on the larger picture of themselves as a family who have shared traditions and memories and who once didn't feel as angry as they now do. Rekindling shades of that recognition without being Pollyanna-ish or overly sentimental is important.

Bear in Mind that Teenaged Clients Usually Understand More than Their Parents Give Them Credit For

Most adolescents understand a lot more about the tensions among family members than their parents give them credit for; they just have a harder time talking about those tensions.

Consider, during early sessions, that the adolescent has a valid perspective hidden beneath a lot of resentment such that it can't show through. Find opportunities in the session to raise this as a possibility, without putting the teenager on the spot. Help her articulate her perspective if she needs your help and seems willing to let you do that. If she doesn't, leave her be for the present.

> Most adolescents understand a lot more about the tensions among family members than their parents give them credit for; they just have a harder time talking about those tensions.

Observe and Comment on Conspicuous Absences Within the Family System

See what's missing: boundaries, respect, compassion, clarity, assertiveness, self-respect, humor, affection, genuineness, directness of communication, and/or relating. Consider what roles the absence(s) might have in the problems the family is presenting, and find ways to introduce that thread of thinking into the consultation. Move the parents toward more compassion or humor or benevolence or firmness if that's what they need more of, *and* if they have the flexibility in their personalities and family styles to accommodate. Teach them how to communicate their worry without becoming overbearing, patronizing, or hysterical. For example:

> "Ed, I know you're used to trying to hammer it in. But you're losing this kid's attention. Tell him simply that you're so terrified of losing him that you can't see straight. I think he can respond better to that than to your 'I'm laying down the law talk.'"

> "Marcia, just tell her that you miss her. That's all. Be the first here to soften and see if your daughter will respond."

Use the Parents' Presence in the Room to State Your Observation About the Teenager that You Can't Comment on Directly to the Teenager

"Mike won't allow us to think that any of this matters to him, will he?" I said softly to the mother of a 16-year-old high school sophomore who was shrugging his way through a conversation about his suicidal thoughts, deteriorating school performance, apparent depression, and chronic pain from a sports-related injury.

"He never does," she replied, looking at her son.

I didn't ask Mike directly because he would only have denied my observation or answered with another shrug. It was more important that I find a way to begin reframing his indifference than it was that he admit being affected by his troubles.

In an initial family session for a 15-year-old girl who, according to her parents, was messing with the wrong crowd, I noticed every one of the mother's questions being sneered at, eye-rolled, or ignored. Neither the girl's mother nor father was saying anything about it, so *I* decided to—but not to the girl herself, which certainly would only have netted a similarly disdainful nonverbal response. I turned to the mother and asked, "Does your daughter always treat your questions with such contempt?"

"Always," came the mother's reply. This gave me an opportunity to introduce the issue of Courtney's attitude, which was an important prelude to discussing the choices she was making regarding friends, school, and the like. Commenting on someone's interpersonal style invariably has the effect of making him or her more self-conscious about it; therefore, another benefit to putting a finer point on the way in which Courtney was responding to her mother was that she could no longer do it as casually in session. Her flippancy subsided quickly, without her ever having been told to change her demeanor.

Be Careful to Position Yourself as in Alignment with Everybody, at the Expense of No One

Move through conflicting accounts without getting caught up in details, facts, or truth. When the parents ask how you're going to understand what to do if you don't know all the facts, calmly say that you're confident that those things important for you to know will become apparent soon enough, and that pressing too early for a coherent account sometimes loses more than it gains."Yeah, well, I guess it all happened something like that," is what I might say to defuse a problem of conflicting accounts and move on to something more useful.

Don't think you have to give kid-glove treatment in order to stay in alignment with everybody. Sometimes saying the unacknowledged but mutually understood truth about a situation can crystallize a working relationship better than anything else the therapist can do in that moment. For example:

- "I don't think Katie expects people to take her sense of entitlement seriously, and I think she's shocked when they do." This cemented a silent alliance between 15-year-old Katie and me, because it spoke to what she knew to be true about herself but could never say.

- "Michael knows he can be a hothead, and I think it surprises him to get away with it." This comment served to settle Michael down in session and subsequently at home, because it acknowledged the power he was wielding through his bluster but also authorized his parents not to respond in their typical ways.

- To the parents of an acting-out boy: "You guys need to do a better job of standing side by side and not letting the other get hung out to dry during these conflicts with Theo. Diane, if Hank starts to withdraw when you confront Theo, go pull him back in. And Hank, if you start to feel like Diane is taking charge too much, tell her to move over and let you in."

- And to Theo: "That's for your parents, but I have something for you. You get a little too self-satisfied watching your parents struggle to deal with your shenanigans. If you have a legitimate point, then speak up and discuss it with them. You can get a little too passive for your own good."

- Do *not* play to the teenager, and guide the parents in not playing to her either.

- Unless . . . the teenager is really trying to help himself. Then, it's not a matter of playing to the teenager but of respecting his experience of the problem and his genuine wish to move beyond it. Asking the teen what he would like out of the therapy, what he thinks has to happen, or what is the one question that you should have but haven't yet asked are good ways to encourage his participation.

Problems in the Consulting Room

Parents Expect You to "Do" Therapy with Their Adolescent while They Observe

Here's a frequent occurrence: You sit down with a family for a first visit, ask an opening question, and watch as the parents turn to their sullen son or daughter, expecting the teen to take over the reins and respond.

I don't think so.

Gail started off her family's first session that way after having dragged her 14-year-old son in to meet with me. Gail and I had spoken briefly on the phone, and I knew that she was unhappy with Drew's recent slide in grades and increasing withdrawal at home. When I asked her what she thought was different for Drew that would account for the changes, she shrugged and said, "I don't know. Why don't you ask him?"

"I don't want to ask him." I said. "I want to know what you think."

"Well, I'm not sure if I know the right reason."

"The right reason doesn't matter to me now as much as understanding how you guys go about trying to figure out problems. This isn't the last time you're going to be concerned about something Drew is or isn't doing. Let me help you problem solve and you'll be that much better off both now and in the future."

"But why aren't you asking him?" Gail wondered, understandably.

"Because no self-respecting adolescent gives away the house that quickly, so I'm not even going to put him on the spot."

Parents Indulge Their Adolescent's Dismissive Attitude in Session

Lonnie and Walt brought their 15-year-old daughter in for me to help. It seems that Kelly got herself caught stealing checks from her family's mailbox and had herself a little shopping spree. Kelly thought this was all no big deal—after all, no one was hurt, and she promised she wouldn't do it again anyway.

She offered no explanation for her actions, no apology, no nothing. She was as cool and glib as you'd ever care to see. Kelly's parents, rather than using her attitude as a communication of disinterest for which she would then be held responsible, tried to solicit her interest and participation. It was a kiss of death for them and their authority. I told them that I found their queries of Kelly too indulgent. I suggested that we move along to discuss in Kelly's presence the worrisome nature of her dismissive attitude.

In another case, Margaret, a single parent of a 13-year-old daughter, arrived distressed and exhausted for her second session. Isabel had refused to go to school that morning, successfully engaged her mother in a verbal duel that escalated into an outright screaming match, convinced her mom to call in sick to work and stay home with her, and then, to top it off, managed to make Margaret feel responsible for the whole mess!

When Margaret asked her daughter why she didn't get out of bed, Isabel's response was that she "couldn't"—that sometimes her body just wouldn't listen to her so it was best just to try another day when she might feel more like getting up. This line of questioning was going nowhere, I thought to myself, and quickly redirected the conversation back to mom and *what she was going to do* the next time her daughter decided she wasn't going to school, rather than what Isabel was feeling that kept her from getting her body up.

Were there real issues making Isabel anxious about school? Sure there were. But Isabel was old enough to be held responsible for communicating directly that she was anxious about something and needed help, and her mother's focus on how Isabel was feeling and the whims of her body served only to affirm Isabel's "belief" that getting out of bed in the morning was not under her voluntary control.

The Adolescent Won't Talk

Parents worry when their kids don't talk in session. They think that talking is a necessary ingredient to a successful therapy. The therapist must help them understand that it is not. When they wonder what role their child *will* play, reply that you don't yet know. Tell them there are many times when the teenager's involvement is minimal, and that often you end up working only with the parents, especially if the adolescent is waiting or needing to be coaxed into joining the process. Explain that if the conversation becomes interesting enough to the teenager, he or she will find some point at which to join in—then you have a genuine participant. Anything short of that is a waste of time and a compromising position for the parent or therapist to take up.

"What if she never says anything?"

"Then she doesn't. You and I get to do all the talking. And all the deciding."

The moment that the therapist allows the viability of the therapy to be contingent on the adolescent's participation, she has vastly limited her options for working with the family. By refusing to define the therapy as needing the adolescent's direct involvement, the therapy is then free to move forward in any number of variously configured, constructive ways.

Not only is it not necessary to talk with the teenager in order for therapy to get started or take place, there are some advantages to choosing not to directly address the teen in the beginning:

- It reduces pressure on the adolescent to talk, which has the secondary effect of making it easier for them to do so should they wish to.

- It disorients the adolescent because she very possibly was expecting to be peppered with questions by the therapist; it's another way of communicating that the therapy will be different and not predictable.

- It assesses the flexibility and maneuverability of the parents. Will they be able to follow your leads about communication and power, and not feel compelled to solicit their teen's involvement? Or do they keep plying him with questions, still trying to make something happen?

- It takes the wind out of the sails of a defiant teen who might have been expecting to use her silence to thwart the process.

- It offers the teenager an opportunity to hear what the adults' concerns are and change on his own before doing it in response to the adult's requests or injunctions.

Creating family session environments in which adolescents want to talk and be involved is a relatively simple task, as long as the therapist doesn't get too concerned about "making" it happen. Therapies that are hitting the mark will naturally elicit participation or, occasionally, the intent but silent interest of a teenager who is relieved to be seeing critical matters addressed between therapist and parent(s). Therapists may have to help a kid join the discussion after a session or two of silence, so that his participation

> Not directly addressing the teenaged client in the beginning of the therapy disorients the adolescent because she very possibly was expecting to be peppered with questions by the therapist; it's another way of communicating that the therapy will be different and not predictable.

is not made into a big deal. I'll sometimes try to find a quick and easy question for the adolescent who looks ready to be more directly involved but needs a subtle entrance ramp into the conversation. I might, for instance, ask the adolescent for the location of an event under discussion by her parents, and then revert back to my conversation with the parents. This way, her first comment is unremarkable and doesn't put any attention on the fact that she is now talking.

Chapter Eight

Helping Parents to Manage Their Volatile Adolescent

If we think we have our hands full for the hour we work with these kids in therapy, we only need to think of the parents who wrestle every day with their teen's volatility, indifference, or opposition. Counseling difficult teenagers and their parents requires a sensitivity to what these parents have been going through that is different from or more extreme than what parents of adolescents who display the more moderate and normal range of emotional and behavioral problems experience.

Helping the parents of these more troubled teens often becomes a matter of:

- Reinstilling faith that change is possible.

- Rekindling their benevolence, which may have soured over the months of wrangling with their teenaged child.

- Restoring their sense of authority.

- Helping them find constructive ways to balance support and discipline.

- Assisting them to understand that their child may not know how to ask for help in the "right" way.

- Helping them follow through in the face of the monkey wrenches their kids will try to throw in the way of firm, effective, compassionate parenting.

How Interpersonal Problems Turn Into Behavioral Problems

Lost Opportunities

So many behavioral problems among adolescents begin as interpersonal ones, but parents get so overwhelmed at the prospect of solving them in interpersonal terms that they try to avoid it and instead address the problems literally and with discipline only. Parents of distressed, and especially angry, teens often have trouble talking directly to their children about their concerns. They may fear another emotional outburst, sarcastic tirade, or bout of mutual alienation, and begin to lose confidence in their ability to parent effectively. Others are so worn out from weeks, months, or perhaps even years of conflict that they no longer have the energy, wherewithal, or desire to keep working so hard to change things around. Still others are limited by their belief that the answer to the problem lies in exerting more control over a situation that has already deserted their realm of power.

Following are several ways in which families characteristically don't deal with the emotional factors in their adolescent's behavioral problems.

> So many behavioral problems among adolescents begin as interpersonal ones, but parents get so overwhelmed at the prospect of solving them in interpersonal terms that they try to avoid it and instead address the problems literally and with discipline only.

Denial/Avoidance

The Glick family blanched at the idea that their family was one that didn't talk to one another about their problems. "Oh, we're not that kind of family," defended the mother, Lil. "We'd love to talk about such things but you have to understand, Janet, we're a very busy family. Scott has soccer three days a week, and the twins are really involved at the high school, and Lenny is at the office until eight or nine each night. Besides, teenagers never like to tell their parents anything anyway."

"Says who?" I asked.

That was my first attempt to break up this family's fixed beliefs about the ways things were and needed to be. I figured that maybe if I could get them to entertain the idea that the teenage thing was a myth, or that it could become a myth for their own family at least, then perhaps they could make a myth out of the idea that they were a family that was too busy to talk.

The Butlers were another family that didn't recognize how they let everyday opportunities to connect with one another slip away from them under the guise of "Dad's not a talker." When I asked them in an initial session what kinds of things 14-year-old Rachel and her dad talked about together, the reply from mom was, "Oh, Rachel and her dad don't talk very much. Gerry's not really the talking kind."

My reaction was that maybe Gerry wasn't the talking kind but his daughter was. Why can't he learn? And if it's really so hard for him to talk, is there anything he can think of to substitute for that avenue of connection between him and his daughter?

Bullying Feelings

Some parents have such a hard time listening to and accepting their distressed adolescent's feelings once they are finally expressed that they just run the feelings over with platitudes, empty reassurances, and other forms of dismissal. Then they wonder why their kid "never tells them anything."

Matt, father of two adolescent boys, was brought up in a family where pennies were pinched and everyone was made annoyingly aware of just how lucky they were to have anything. Birthday presents, holiday gifts, and even extra snacks were doled out with such an expectation of gratitude on the parts of both parents that Matt and his brothers came to resent the whole thing. When Matt's 16-year-old son would begin complaining about his lot in life, as kids do, it touched such a nerve in his dad that all Matt could manage to say in response was, "Don't start walking around here with that chip on your shoulder again, pal. Quit complaining. You don't know how good you have it."

Well, Peter knew. But everyone has a time when "as good as it can be" isn't going to be good enough. And while some of Peter's beefing was hardwired into adolescence, Matt's defensive response gave him no opportunity to look past the face value of his son's comment and use it as an opportunity to discuss what Peter might really have been unhappy about in his life.

"Matt," I interrupted one time in session when he jumped down Peter's throat after Peter complained about excessive responsibilities, "no teenager ever thinks he or she has it good enough. It's a rite of passage into adolescence. But some of Peter's complaints might be legitimate, and we'll never know if you keep giving him the message that he shouldn't complain. Your son's not a bad kid and sometimes has some very good points. When you jump on him you lose the opportunity to hear something that may have merit, and you also lose the chance to teach him how to distinguish between things he should be complaining about and things he maybe shouldn't be."

Fear of Getting Too Angry

Some adolescents have learned to push their parents' buttons so well when they do press issues that the parents wind up feeling angrier and more out of control than the child.

"I can't stand to argue with him anymore," one despairing parent confided in me after her son walked out of my office on both of us. "He knows that I feel guilty about being a single mom and always manages to turn a situation around so that I end up feeling even more guilty—like his problems are all my fault or something!"

Fear of the Adolescent Becoming Out of Control

Some parents worry that their adolescent can become so out of control that she could become physically destructive or even dangerous to herself or another. That's what stopped Nina's parents in their tracks every time.

"The last time we told Nina that she couldn't go to a concert she'd be planning to attend, she spent the whole night in her room cutting up her arms with a pocket knife. We didn't even find out about it until the morning. We just can't take that chance again, but we have to set some limits, don't we?" her mom wondered.

Protecting Other Family Members

Many times parents drop an issue in order to prevent other family members from being drawn into the problems they are having with the one child, or from having to deal with the miserable fallout from conflict. Ken's parents did this for years, before they learned that the gains were short-lived and served only to increase Ken's control over the family's activities.

"Ken's tantrums were not only disrupting our lives but the lives of his three brothers as well," said Kim's mother, describing her son's tendency to strike out physically at his parents when confronted, and never think twice about causing a scene in restaurant, parking lots, or family functions. "Sometimes we just drop the whole issue because we can't bear to have him keep carrying on."

Fear of Saying the "Wrong" Thing and Inciting a Bad Reaction

The parents of 15-year-old Maria were desperate to reach their daughter and stem the flood of her angry outbursts and destructive tantrums. But each time they'd try to talk with her, Maria would get angrier and more destructive. Worried that being firmer with her or more frank about their concerns would agitate their daughter even more, Maria's parents opted for quiet reproaches, hoping that would engender more cooperation. Her mother explained, "I know I come off as a softie sometimes, but I keep thinking that by being more patient, she'll eventually become a little more reasonable."

She didn't.

Sixteen-year-old Julie had been holding her parents hostage for months with her sullen silence, withdrawal, and sarcastic outbursts. Fearful of "making things worse," or of "upsetting Julie even more," Debra and Nate, her parents, became paralyzed with self-consciousness in their efforts to manage and talk to her. Nate told me, "If we try to ask her what's wrong, she snaps our heads off or storms up to her room. If we try and just make easy conversation, like 'How's school?' she looks at us as if we're idiots. And forget it if we try to tell her what to do, or what time to be home! She'll start screaming that we don't trust her and that we're the cause of all her problems. And she won't even tell us what those problems are. She seems so miserable. All we want to do is help. . . ."

Feeling Too Beleaguered/Tired/Hopeless

Seventeen-year-old Ray had been running his dad ragged for the past six months and was about to lose this last and most vital support left in his dwindling circle of friends and fans. Charming, gregarious, kind even, this boy had shown no mercy on his family in his quest for bigger thrills and more fanciful escapes from capture. Ray repeatedly ignored curfew, waved off groundings, and informed no one of his afterschool whereabouts. Now he'd been caught smashing neighbors' mailboxes, smoking marijuana, and joyriding. His dad had tried everything he knew to do to help his son. He sat in a therapist's office, threw up his hands, and said, "I'm sick and tired of worrying about his well-being more than he is. I have his younger brother to worry about, you know, and he's too good to be getting the short end of the stick here."

Too Controlling to Tolerate Candid Discussions with Their Adolescent

"I want to know what she has done to advance her goals of graduating from high school," Lydia's father informed me, sternly pointing his finger in his 17-year-old daughter's direction. She sat shrunken-looking and timid in a corner of the room.

"I'm not convinced those are her goals," I replied.

"Well, they ought to be."

"They might ought to have been, but they aren't now." I looked squarely at the father and shrugged.

"Well, then, I hope at least you've been talking to her about her cigarette smoking!" he demanded to know. I looked at him and sighed.

How often have you sat in session with a family in trouble and thought to yourself: What a shame it is that they won't let themselves help one another . . . ? If only the daughter would let her dad say something nice without rolling her eyes. If only the mother would stop playing the walking wounded game and deal with her family as an adult.

When I find myself in that situation I look for ways to say something to the people in the room to help them see that they've become too acclimated to their tendency to hide from one another, or too complacent with what appears to be such a modest level of emotional intimacy. I recognize that close relating isn't everybody's cup of tea, and respect a person's wish to solve the problem (if possible) without a focus on developing warmer relationships among the family members, but sometimes the people are so lost and far away from each other that they don't even recognize what it is I'm describing as not being present in their lives.

❋

Helping Too-Careful Parents

Helping parents who are too tentative or self-conscious about interacting with their reactive adolescent children often involves inspiring confidence in their ability to make "decent-enough" decisions (they don't have to be perfect) as a parent, and manage competently (it doesn't have to be expertly) whatever distressing situation arises. Parents also benefit from learning that their confidence in themselves and willingness to take reasonable relationship risks that are guided by reason and judgment serve to decrease the likelihood of the adolescent acting up and testing the limits, rather than increasing it. The following are specific measures a therapist can take with such parents to help them better guide and redirect their troubled adolescent child.

> Parents also benefit from learning that their confidence in themselves and willingness to take reasonable relationship risks that are guided by reason and judgment serve to decrease the likelihood of the adolescent acting up and testing the limits, rather than increasing it.

Emoting for the Parent

The emotional neutralization of parents of belligerent kids is a term coined by Jerome Price in his book, *Power and Compassion: Working With Difficult Adolescents and Their Abused Parents,** to describe what happens when parents stop responding with appropriate emotion to their adolescent's behavior. Whether because of guilt, conflict avoidance, or demoralization, these parents can no longer muster the affect, and instead react with muted emotions that tell the teenager only that he is getting his way yet one more time. One valuable intervention a therapist can offer a parent in this situation is to emote for them the reaction they should be having, and that the kid should be hearing.

Terry and Steve brought in their 13-year-old son, Jeremy, because of his escalating violent and belligerent behavior within the home over the past couple of months. Most of this behavior had been directed toward Terry, who then would call Steve at work to complain about all the awful things Jeremy was doing.

---

*Price, J. A. (1996). *Power and compassion: Working with difficult adolescents and abused parents.* New York: Guilford.

"Why won't he listen to me?" she repeatedly asked Steve whenever she called, not realizing how much she was undermining her own power when she depended on him to do the disciplining later on, after he came home from work.

I asked the parents to describe for me a recent episode, and they picked one from two days before where Jeremy had shouted nasty things to his mom all the way home from hockey practice. When they happened to mention that Terry had taken Jeremy over to the video store later that day to pick a flick, I half jumped out of my seat. "Are you telling me that you took this kid to the video store after having spent that whole ride home from the game being called names!? I don't believe it, and I bet even he (I pointed toward Jeremy) couldn't believe it when it was happening." I turned to Jeremy. "Am I right about that?" I asked.

"Yes," came back Jeremy's bewildered response.

Once these parents saw how ridiculous it was that Terry took Jeremy video shopping after his outburst, it turned a tide for them and gave Terry the support she needed to say no the next time, which began to curb Jeremy's appetite for car ride brawls.

Patti was brought in to me by her parents after her school counselor notified them about cuts on Patti's arm, which were reported by another student in her school. Remarkably, no one had actually seen her arms. Patti refused to show them to anyone, and no adult had insisted. So here we were sitting in my office with a sullen, sarcastic girl of 16 whose arms were supposedly pretty sliced up, and parents who were too restrained to insist on seeing them.

"No one has asked Patti to show them how bad or not so bad the cuts are?" I asked.

"She won't let us see them," replied Patti's dad.

"Dan, your daughter reportedly cut herself. We don't know if it's scratches or more. She's 16. She's not talking to anyone. She's not in a position to be deciding whether or not anyone can check her out. It doesn't have to be a big deal, or any more intrusive than a glance by one person, and she can choose. But you and Deirdre must act."

"I know," Deirdre said. "I guess that, it's just that, she's already so angry at us and I didn't want to push anything and make it worse. . . . Plus, I didn't want her to see how upset I was."

"Patti can be permitted to see how upset this all makes you, and she'll be all right. There are consequences for doing things that scare people and they include having to witness the pain your actions wind up putting your loved ones through. Patti needs to know that she can scare you, but she can't scare you off. She may not want to talk about her cutting right now, but I think there are other things that you and Dan can do to support her through this period."

There are times when it's better for the family to have less, not more, affect as their emotional reaction. I supervised the case of a 15-year-old girl who had just been discharged from the hospital following a serious bout of depression and anorexia nervosa. She had been a star pupil and field hockey player and, when making the unavoidable comparisons between her earlier level of academic and social functioning her and current level, had become depressed all over again.

Lisa's parents were more alarmed by the posthospital depression than by the earlier one. Operating under the mistaken impression that Lisa's discharge meant that all the pain of before was gone and now Lisa would make a "fresh start" to her life, they denied their daughter the opportunity to quietly mourn her loss of the past few months, and deal with her sadness over what was an undeniable—but not necessarily permanent—loss in her level of functioning. They tried to cheerlead her into feeling happy and, when that failed, got impatient and histrionic in their pleas for her to "lighten up already and see the good side to things!"

I told Lisa's parents that I thought the monster wasn't their daughter's depression, but rather everyone's intense efforts to get her out of it. Lisa's parents were stunned. "Let her be depressed," I advised. "After all, why shouldn't she be? She's smart enough to know what she's missed for the time being, and, frankly, I'd be more worried about her if she weren't feeling down." I went on to explain that any kind of denial over how this was affecting her wasn't going to make anyone feel better, and that when Lisa began once again to feel she could recreate the life for herself that she successfully led before, she would start to feel better.

In Session, Point Out to Parents Ways in Which They Are Trying Too Hard and Unproductively to Avoid Conflict

Ethan wasn't even close to convincing his dad that he hadn't known the driver's-side door of his car was off the frame. And this was after he'd already admitted to his dad that he had backed the car with its door open into the oak tree lining their driveway. Ethan's father said, "Ethan, the door doesn't shut. You couldn't even have sat in the car without knowing it was off the frame."

"No, Dad, honest, I looked all over for damages and didn't see any. I thought the car was fine, and that's why I didn't see any reason to say anything. The car looked fine to me then. Really."

As Ethan tried to weasel out of yet one more responsibility, Ethan's mom, ever the mediator between her hot-headed husband and son, ever the keeper of the peace, rushed in to reframe Ethan's unaccountability as a "misunderstanding." Yikes, I said to myself. The only misunderstanding here is how much Ethan snows her.

"You protect these guys too much, Ellen. Ethan doesn't misunderstand, but he knows that misunderstanding something makes him less accountable than does messing up. When you rescue him with that line, you protect him and his dad from their tempers but rob them of the opportunity to learn to deal with this problem of theirs, and especially Ethan of his."

Help the Parents Articulate What They Fear Would Happen if They Spoke or Acted More Confidently

Then help them to become more comfortable with the repercussions (e.g., conflict, stone silence, self-doubt) or, should the repercussions involve behaviors thought to be very risky (e.g., running away, self-injurious acting out), put into place some type of system so that the event can be managed safely.

"What do you worry would happen were you to say just that?" I ask parents of an out-of-control kid. Following are some sample responses.

Scenario One

"She'd never come out her room. She's already so withdrawn I hate to do anything to make her withdraw more."

"Let her withdraw then, if she chooses. She won't stay in her room forever, and you can't make yourself responsible for her choice of reaction. You'll have to deal with her with-drawal, but you cannot avoid acting and parenting in order to prevent it."

"How would we deal with it?"

"I'd tell Brittany what family events or obligations you expect her to attend, and what the consequences will be if she doesn't. For instance, if she ignores your request to come down for a family meal, or to greet a visiting relative, she loses the car for two days."

"I hate to take things away. What about if I give her extra privileges for doing those things?"

"Then you're bribing. Coming down for meals or to kiss grandma hello are expected behaviors. They shouldn't be rewarded. Do, though, let Brittany know how much you enjoy her company when she does join everyone—if you do. If you don't, because she's sulky or something, tell her that you're so happy to see her around the first floor again that you'll even put up with her being grumpy!"

Scenario Two

"I'm worried he will get angry enough to break something in the house."

"He might, Louise, and then both he and you have to deal with the consequences—you with the loss of something that may be irreplaceable, and he with having to pay restitution, replace the item, and apologize. If it's bad enough, press charges for property damage."

Price notes that a parent's recognition that his or her adolescent is out of control and needs outside intervention, such as the police, can be a critical factor in their getting the child the help needed.

Scenario Three

"It sounds weird, but I'm worried she'll blurt out something that I don't want to hear or know about. Like drugs or sex or something. I'm worried she'll try and get back at me by shocking me."

"She might, but you need to become unshockable. It's better that you know about these things, anyway. Then you have the opportunity to hold her accountable because you can ask Sheila to make changes in the behaviors you see as unfit for her.

Scenario Four

"I'm worried that if I raise my voice or press the issue he'll get out of control and become wild or even violent."

"That's why you have 911 on your phone. You must get comfortable with the prospect of having to use 911 and he must know that, without your using it as a threat. Otherwise he will continue to hold you hostage to your fear. Or, make sure you have a person with you—friend, brother, co-worker—who will be present when you confront your son, and who can restrain him if the need arises."

"This sounds so programmed."

"It might need to be. You need to set the situation up in whatever manner allows you to parent in the way your son needs you to parent and be firm with him. If it's programmed or unspontaneous, then so be it."

Scenario Five

"I'm worried she'll start having those terrible thoughts of killing herself again."

The important thing is for the parents to realize that they cannot allow anything the teenager threatens to do or is capable of doing to stop the parents from parenting. They need to know that they should get whatever help they require and use all available support and resources so that they are free to act and talk in the ways they believe are necessary.

"Then you act as you need to, and follow it up with round-the-clock monitoring. You say, 'Every time we have one of these blowouts you become despondent. I worry about that but cannot let it stop me from trying to do what's best, so I've instituted some safety measures. Uncle Joe is spending the next few days with us to help me make sure you're ok.'"

The important thing is for the parents to realize that they cannot allow anything the teenager threatens to do or is capable of doing to stop the parents from parenting. They need to know that they should get whatever help they require and use all available support and resources so that they are free to act and talk in the ways they believe are necessary.

Coach Parents in Session as They Confront or Otherwise Address Their Teenager

Examples could include the following:

> "Leslie, turn to William now and explain to him what those consequences are going to be. If he's sitting there telling you basically to get lost, inform him how that will cost him. If you wait until later, you are letting him know that it's acceptable for him to address you like that."

"Warren, don't even begin to debate that one. I'd simply inform Ashley now that it's nonnegotiable. You and Wendy have already told her she cannot go and why. And despite her countenance I truly believes she understands completely but is trying to appeal to your egalitarian side. Entering into a discussion legitimizes her contesting of the parameter. Stick to your guns."

Model Speaking and Relating to the Teenager in Session in Ways that Are Appealing and Empathic Without Being "Careful"

Desensitize a family to the candor and forthrightness if they are too tentative with one another.

Help the Parents Comb Through Their Own Histories and Find Times When They Were Able to Parent With Greater Authority and Effectiveness

Ask solution-focused questions,* such as:

- When have you ever been able to do this?

- What was different about you? About your spouse? Your child? Your circumstances? Your lifestyle?

- What's one thing you feel you need to do or have in order to feel better prepared to do this job?

---

*de Shazer, S. (1985). *Keys to solution in brief therapy.* New York: Norton; de Shazer, S. (1988). *Clues: Investigating solutions in brief therapy.* New York: Norton; DeJong, P., & Berg, I. K. (1998). *Interviewing for Solutions.* New York: Brooks/Cole.

- What can we do here today that would help to accomplish that?

- What else do you need?

Maybe the parent says she needs a husband's support. Help her to ask that of him, or underscore her need to him yourself and comment on his not having supported her enough.

Darcy and Bill brought in their 14-year-old daughter, Nadia, for therapy. Within minutes it became apparent that Darcy got negligible support from Bill in handling their out-of-control daughter. Nadia would arrange for friends to pick her up despite being grounded and Bill, home without Darcy, would let her go off with them. When I asked why he let her go, he said, "What else could I have done? Her friends were already there." I was incredulous.

On another occasion Bill frankly admitted to not restraining his daughter from activities that Darcy had prohibited her from engaging in or that they both discouraged. He told me, "I just don't want the hassle, to tell you the truth." Bill was a depressed, passive-aggressive man whose enormous anger at his wife and inability to manage conflict manifested in his near-complete disavowal of parenting duties. With Darcy left to put the foot down, it was no wonder that Nadia and Darcy fought constantly and that Nadia and her dad "got along great," according to both father and daughter. "I don't have any problems with her," shrugged Bill.

I rejoined, "How are you so comfortable leaving your wife out to dry like that?" He shrugged, glib and aloof. Darcy stared at her husband. I continued, "Look, Bill, Darcy needs your help. And your daughter needs you to help your wife, too. They're both bearing the brunt of you taking the easy way out of this."

With that bit of support, Darcy took over, saying assertively but without being shrill, melodramatic, or threatening, "Bill, I do need you right there beside me on all these matters, to back me up. Better yet, I need you to initiate some of the discipline, too. If you disagree with what I think, that's fine, but do it privately and come back with some kind of other idea—don't just dismiss mine out of hand."

Finally, for the first time in the 3 weeks we'd been meeting, I saw this man take something seriously. And a phone call several weeks later disclosed a "100% improvement" in Nadia, according to Darcy, which I believe could only have happened by there being a considerable improvement in how she and Bill were managing their parenting responsibilities to their daughter and to each other.

Helping Beleaguered Parents

Ask the Parents Directly if They Have Been Feeling Overwhelmed

You may feel as if you're speaking the obvious, but many people feel better just having their fatigue recognized by an outside party. Sometimes it even helps them not to wear their beleaguered status on their sleeve quite so much.

I remember sitting in session with a single mom and her 15-year-old daughter. Two weekends previously, Amanda had been caught at a party with older kids. There had been no supervision but plenty of alcohol. Amanda had spent the ensuing two weeks shunning, disrespecting, and withdrawing from her mother. In this first session, Amanda's mom looked too exhausted to do anything more strenuous than sit on the couch across the room from me. Meanwhile, Amanda challenged her mother's concerns and limits brazenly, complaining that she was overprotective and "too neurotic" about alcohol. Gretchen stared down at the floor, her shoulders sagging and spirits deflated. She could hardly respond, and when she did, Amanda quipped back so fast and incisively it made both Gretchen's and my head spin.

I excused Amanda from the session, sat back down, and said to Gretchen something about how exhausted she seemed. Gretchen immediately burst into tears, then followed up by speaking about how hard it had been for her to keep on going, by herself as a single parent with no support from Amanda's father, in the face of her daughter's unrelenting arguing. I spent the rest of the session helping Gretchen figure out how she could marshal the reserves to take care of matters as she needed to. This was more useful than meeting with Amanda.

For Gretchen, the beleaguerment came from feeling beaten down over time, having to manage problems with negligible support, and perceiving her inability to have any effect on her troubled daughter. For other parents, it might be that they are so angry that they have partly given up, or that they are so hopeless about the situation that their despair overshadows their natural commitment to help. Making these problems overt can help these parents feel like they can find solutions and forgive themselves for what are almost always normal and expectable feelings given what such parents are trying to manage.

One case I supervised involved a mother of a 16-year-old boy whose disrespectful behavior and cantankerous attitude over the years had driven her to exhaustion and near despair. The therapist found the mother strikingly discompassionate and inflexible regarding working collaboratively with her son, Carl.

"I've had it," the mom told the therapist working the case. "I'm tired of being the only one who cares how this is all going to work out. I gave him lots of chances, and now he's got to me meet me all the way!"

I recommended to this therapist that she focus on three points with the mom:

1. Express empathy for her situation and an apprecia-
    tion of how it could drive anyone to feel like throw-
    ing up her hands and saying she's done all she could
    or wanted to.

2. Communicate candidly how her unforgiving attitude
    might come across to her son, and what the pros and
    cons of that would be—for example, he might begin
    to take her more seriously but he also might turn off
    completely, especially if he were about to come to the
    table with something.

3. Articulate her choices for her, and help her decide
    which path she preferred to take at this time, and
    what to do if she changed her mind.

Assess How Resilient the Parents Are

How can their efforts to help be resuscitated? What do the parents need in order to feel prepared to do more? You can ask the following questions to help remobilize the parents:

*   Do they feel as if they have reached bottom? Do they
    need to let the problem ride for a few days in order
    to take a break and then come back to it refreshed?

- Do they want to meet with other parents in similar situations? Are there groups in the community to which they can be referred for that, and/or other support services available?

- Is there someone—a sister, an aunt, a close friend, and so on—who can help out at the home for a couple of weeks?

Connect the Parents to Other Resources (Extended Family, Community Groups, Social Service Agencies) That Could Be Available for Support

This is especially important for a single-parent family. Martha Straus's book *Violence in The Lives Of Adolescents** is especially useful for its lists of organizations and groups available to parents. Particularly noteworthy are the following:

- Parents Anonymous—for parents who can be abusive.

- Because I Love You—the support group for families dealing with truancy, substance abuse, and defiance.

- *The Self-Help Sourcebook* by White and Madara.[†]

- Youth volunteer services.

- Mentor programs for adolescents.

---

*Straus, M. B. (1994). *Violence in the lives of adolescents*. New York: Norton.
[†]White, B. J., & Madara, E. J. (1992). *The self-help sourcebook*. Denville, NJ: Saint Clares-Riverside Medical Center.

Ask What You Can Do Specifically in Session to Help Them Feel Less Beleaguered

Among the different things that the therapy can offer are:

- Hope that things can change.

- Support for the parents.

- A new approach or perspective.

- Direct intervention with the adolescent.

- Intervention with the extended family.

- Indirect intervention by coordinating strategies with the school.

- Permission for the parents to let the problem be more the kid's issue than theirs.

Evoke Appreciation and Compassion from the Adolescent for his Parents' Struggle with the Problems, Even Though He May Disagree with Them about the Matter Itself

Some examples of what you could say are:

> "You know, Nicholas, you've been pushing your own agenda so ferociously for the past few weeks that I don't think you realize the effect all this has had on your folks. You laugh and get sarcastic when they mention how tired they are of all the fighting. I know you don't agree with their point of view, but I think it's only humane that you recognize that these never-ending battles take their toll on your parents, too. Nobody's having a good time here."

> "Melanie, I actually think your dad is more scared than mad, but I don't know that he trusts he can protect you just by being scared. I think he feels he needs to be mad in order to get your attention. Convince him that he doesn't, and see if you both can figure a way out of all this arguing."

You could also confront the teen:

> "You're losing them, guy," I said to the 16-year-old boy who repeatedly rejected his parents' overtures of help for his depression and bad temper. "They'll hang in there with you over the long run, but others may not."

Helping Controlling Parents

Help Parents Become Less Defensive about Their Need to Control, so that They Can Consider Ways to Alter How They Manage Affairs with Their Adolescent Children

Help parents feel less defensive about their overcontrolling tendencies by reframing those tendencies (if appropriate) as benevolences run amok. Discuss with the parents the possibility that maintaining a sense of control over the circumstances in their children's lives may have felt like the only reliable option, even though they knew the costs and limitations. Maybe the overvaluation of control was an heirloom handed down by their family legacies, or maybe it was something borne of their own character or personal history. Helping them have some compassion for a quality in their personality that has proved less useful than believed can help them to feel less protective about it. The parents can then more easily hear a recommendation from you about changing how they think about control with regard to their growing children.

Find a Place to Address the Existentially Human Phenomenon of Having to Give Up Control, and Normalize the Experience for the Parents

How did they learn to put their child on the school bus for the first time? Let her sleep over at somebody's house? Let him drive?

Explain to parents that the predicament of balancing control over their adolescent's well-being with their adolescent's increasing need for independence and autonomy challenges their customary way of navigating the world. Everyone addresses this predicament in a different way. What is theirs?

Help the Parents Locate a Handful of Specific Ways in Which They Can Begin to Relinquish Control, and Encourage Them to Use Each Other for Feedback and Support

Suggest to the parents that they discuss with one another their reactions to letting go, no matter how silly they may feel talking about the experience. Because many people are not comfortable or familiar with talking about their experiences as they are going through them, give them an example of what that might sound like: "Lila, I don't know, this is weird. A part of me feels like running after her right now and telling her she can't go to the concert tonight, and another part of me is relieved not to get so hung up with everything. But then I worry I'm not doing enough! Do you know what I mean?"

Consider Whether Helping the (Older) Teenager Become More Autonomous and Independent from a Too-Controlling Parent Is a Better Option than Helping the Family Work Through the Problems Together

Sophie was a 17-year-old girl who couldn't be more different from the daughter her parents always dreamed of having. Her parents emphasized good grooming; Sophie purposefully went around unkempt. Her parents were conservative in dress; Sophie wore ripped jeans held together with dozens of safety pins, and sweatshirts whose sleeves had holes in them so that they could be worn as gloves. Her father was an oncologist; Sophie smoked a pack of cigarettes a day. Sophie was an only child, and her parents had enormous trouble accepting her as she was and appreciating her benign individuality.

Sophie's parents chose the wrong tactic for trying to change Sophie: They tried to legislate style and personality, and, in their refusal to ever appreciate her differences, lost any opportunity to gain her interest or even her conciliation in modifying some of her behavior, attire, or demeanor. Sophie's native good judgment, intelligence, and personality were being trampled by her parents' well-meaning but misguided attempts to turn her into the daughter they thought they should have.

The parents were very unhappily married, and interacted bizarrely with one another. Sophie would wither in their presence. I thought it impossible to reconcile the differences in the family, and considered that it would be more useful to Sophie for her to be emotionally emancipated. And so that became the objective of therapy.

I never announced to Sophie that I thought that she should stop trying to listen to what her parents were trying to help her understand about herself and them as a family. I never announced frankly that she should emancipate herself from the family. Instead, I spoke to her about ways in which parents and children who match in some ways but not others make different kinds of decisions about how to grow independent of one another. I explained to her that there were useful messages in her parents' reprimands, and helped her learn to avoid the proselytizing that came along with them. This she learned to do well, and eventually was able to launch herself into young adulthood in relative health.

In another situation, I worked with an 18-year-old girl who had just been released from the hospital following a very serious suicide attempt. Denise's father was extremely controlling, and Denise's mother was obviously too intimidated by his demeanor to provide a counterpoint. Denise's father thought it appropriate that his daughter pay for her hospitalization because, after all, she had made the suicide attempt of her own volition. This was not the first time money had been used to control Denise's behavior, and in family sessions he was unresponsive to reconsideration or redirection. Part of the therapy for Denise was helping her learn to appreciate the ways in which her father was trying to care for her, while simultaneously helping her learn to assert her maturity, independence, and dignity in appropriate ways.

Check for a Problem of Postsession Retribution if You Feel That You're Not Getting a Whole Story in Session

When I find children or adolescents being unusually quiet in session, or looking over at a parent to assess reactions to what they are saying, I begin to wonder about what happens after sessions in which they might have said the "wrong thing." Some families are very private and have strict codes about which laundry gets aired and which doesn't, even though they are asking for help. Kids try to stay within the bounds but are sometimes conflicted with their wish to speak the truth and get help for their family or themselves. If I suspect there is concern on a child's or adolescent's part about after-session retribution for lapses in privacy, I'll look to introduce the concept without personalizing it to the family until and unless it becomes apparent that such a problem actually does exist. Some examples include:

> "I have no idea if this is relevant here, but I will tell you something I've been wondering. Whenever the pieces to a situation don't all fit together, or it seems like something is missing from the puzzle, I'll consider that I don't yet have all the information. Of course sometimes it is all there and I'm just missing the boat, but on occasion I've found that I don't have all the pieces in front of me and it's because the family is shy about telling me everything I need to know. Or maybe some members are shy and others aren't but they're worried that the ones who are shy will be upset if the others fill me in. It can be quite a dilemma for a family who wants help but is afraid to let the therapist get to know them."

> "Barry, I know you mean well but I've got to tell you something. The way you hold court here in, I'd be afraid to say much of anything if I were your daughter. Your disapproval packs a wallop with your kids, and I can't imagine that you wouldn't disapprove of some of the ways in which your daughter might describe how she thinks these problems have come

about. But I think it's important that we hear them, and I think also we may find that they have merit as well."

Help Parents to Be Less Domineering in Their Relations and Communications With Their Adolescent by Giving Immediate Feedback as Opportunities Arise in Session

Some examples could include:

To a domineering father who thinks he's saying it differently: "I know your mean well, but I think it is still more of the same."

"Ouch. In the ballpark, Marcos, but still heavy-handed." Then, to the child: "What did you think?"

"If I were your kid, Gloria, what you just said would be good enough to make me want to take out the trash for the next six months!"

When a therapist is successful in helping a parent to better manage or support their troubled adolescent, she helps everyone in the family—client, siblings, spouse. Moving families from states of discord, alienation, or disabling anger or depression toward order, dignity, and compassion is no small feat, and a real gift. Moving teenagers from scorn, defeatism, hopelessness, belligerence, or self-destruction to curiosity, contemplation, engagement, and modulation is just plain magic.

But magic can be real and replicable. It has protocol and purpose. It happens when a person connects with another in such an uncounterfeited way that the attention on each other is full, trusting, and expectant. Psychotherapy can house this phenomenon, but it's much too rich to stay circumscribed to a therapist's office. Perhaps our most important job is to make sure it doesn't.

Index